THE UNINTENDED CONSEQUENCES

Family and Community, the Victims of Isolated Poverty

To Mafara with many thanks

James G. Banks and Peter S. Banks

Jim Banks

Peter Banks

W9-ATZ-338

University Press of America,® Inc.
Dallas · Lanham · Boulder · New York · Oxford

This book is lovingly dedicated to Peggy Banks, wife and mother.

Contents

Tables

Foreword

In the summer of his first year as Secretary of Housing and Urban Development, Henry G. Cisneros was inspired by a lecture given in the spring of 1993 at Howard University titled, "Our Social Immune System: Building Supportive Environments for African-American Families in Public Housing."

James G. Banks delivered that lecture and made a persuasive case that housing policy that was based on a purely physical focus without regard to the concentration of very poor, mainly single-headed families was doomed to fail. He began his analysis by the simple and incontrovertible assertion that although fifty years had produced dramatically better housing, "many young people are insecure and despairing because the comfort and security of family and community have been lost." Banks' sources flowed from a rich stream of thinkers, from Aristotle to William J. Wilson, John Gardner, and Luc DeShepper, and coalesced in the proposition that the elemental forces of family, neighborhood, and community are sufficient to provide the "social immune system" to ward off despair and build hope even amidst poverty. However, the isolation of the poor from those forces, he asserted, would leave the young, in Aristotle's phrase, like the "timeless, lawless, heartless one."

Through a unique collaboration between Jim Banks and his son Peter, this book amplifies Banks' thesis using careful documentation of housing policy since the 1930s interspersed with a vivid firsthand account of his years of service sustaining his beloved community of Anacostia.

The Banks' vision spurred the Cisneros/Clinton administration to move beyond shelter to community-building. Using technical changes in the rules governing public housing, the administration pointed to a future in which a mixed-income housing policy would allow the very poor, the working poor, and the rising middle class to take charge, build community, and knock down the walls isolating the poor.

There are hopeful signs that these policies are working. Bruce Katz of the Brookings Institute has pointed to the 2000 Census, which reports that cities across America have experienced a dramatic decline in the concentration of black poverty.

More study is needed to understand fully what has produced these hopeful changes. For example, one cannot ignore a major decline in crime during the same decade in which housing policy aggressively moved away from the over-concentrating patterns of the past. Whether the rebirth of community and the ameliorating immunizing support systems Jim Banks describes so poignantly will return remains to be seen. Most of us feel that it is but a dream. This book and Jim Banks' service to community suggest it is more than a dream.

> George Latimer
> Distinguished Visiting Professor
> Urban Studies
> Macalester College
> Saint Paul, Minnesota
> September, 2003

Preface

I have spent more than fifty years of my life participating in and observing public efforts to improve the housing conditions of the urban poor. My experiences with government housing programs for the poor began in 1945 when I became an interviewer of applicants for public housing in Washington, DC. It ended in 1974 when I served simultaneously as Executive Director of the National Capital Housing Authority, Historic Preservation Officer, and Administrator of the Model Cities Program.

Since retiring from an active role in government more than thirty years ago, I have continued to observe, with deep interest and some trepidation, the changes that have come to characterize the public housing program in most large American cities, and particularly Washington, DC. Since my retirement I have spent many volunteer hours in Anacostia in the Southeast area of Washington, DC, where I was born. I was aware of the changes in housing from single family houses to apartments and row houses, but I had not realized that much of the population was not active either in local churches or civic associations that had been so strong when I had lived there. As I continued my work with groups in Anacostia, it became clear that the sense of community that I had known so many years before had been lost. It is this experience that has led me to write this book.

Written with my son, Peter, this book is an effort to identify those factors that changed both the mission and performance of public housing over the course of its more-than-seventy-year history. This book is an effort to help readers understand some of the unintended consequences that emerge when the poorest of the poor are isolated.

These issues are controversial. If there is a broader understanding among the general population of the causes of problems in urban areas, we can help to avoid public policies and programs that carry the certain consequences of incivility.

This is not a report of empirical study, but rather an offering of historical facts as well as first-hand accounts of the programs and policies that helped to shape the way American society views the urban poor. We offer our conclusions and recommendations, which urge an intense and committed effort by public policy leaders, academics, and the general public to understand fully the causes of our urban problems, and thus develop the ability to remedy existing conditions and avoid them in the future. It is our hope that this book will bring agreement that our society must eliminate public policies and programs that cause the erosion of the normal instinct of all human beings to embrace families and communities.

James G. Banks
Washington, DC, 2003

Acknowledgements

The authors are especially grateful to Peggy F. Banks, wife of James and mother of Peter, for encouraging the writing of this book and for typing the drafts and the final manuscript. Most of all we are grateful for her influence in minimizing the misunderstandings and disagreements of father and son as they struggled to produce this book.

A special thanks is also given to Richard English, Ph.D., Dean of the School of Social Work at Howard University, for providing office space and for inviting James to serve as the School's 1993 Cosby Visiting Scholar. This produced a lecture titled, "Our Social Immune System: Building Supportive Environments for African American Families in Public Housing."

Special thanks to Eugene Ford and Joseph Horning, both promoters of strong communities and civil environments in the many housing developments they own and manage in Washington, DC, for their financial contributions to the studies that were essential to the writing of this book. Our gratitude also goes to the Community Preservation and Development Corporation and Leslie Steen for providing office space as we completed the first draft of this book.

Thank you to public housing officials, particularly Terri Moorcroft, in Pittsburgh, Pennsylvania; Newark, New Jersey; Baltimore, Maryland; and Washington, DC, who all cordially provided information and, in many cases, interviews with the authors. These officials also made it possible for the authors to visit with public housing residents and staff whose experiences were invaluable in understanding the special problems of public housing tenants who bore the brunt of the incivility that their isolated environment produced.

Special acknowledgment is given to the influence of women in Washington, DC, whose understanding of the needs of their neighbors fueled the dawning of a new environment where hope and commitment have led to achievement. They include Brenda Richardson, who served as the first executive director of the Anacostia/Congress Heights Partnership; Margaret O'Bryon, who served as its first Consultant Advisor; and Jackie Massey, a public housing resident who had the vision of positive change and refused to move out of a largely vacant public housing development until the Housing Authority took the first steps to provide a healthy social environment for its residents. Other residents, Dorothea Farrell, Myrtle Loughery, Gloria Thurman, and Brenda Wright, as this book is written, lead their communities in improving the educational achievements of children and reducing crime. Neither Brenda Jones nor Hannah Hawkins live in public housing, but they both have devoted their lives to helping children and families reject the corrosive impact of isolated public housing environments and begin community relationships that grow stronger each day. These women have produced the evidence that when neighbors work unselfishly together, they can overcome the most unyielding problems of urban living.

Thank you to Marcy Thorner, The Grammar Guru, for her keen editorial insight, and to Amy Lee for helping us get the books we needed.

Many thanks also to the US Library of Congress for providing both office space and research resources. The staff of the Washingtoniana Room of the Martin Luther King Library in Washington, DC, was most helpful in our research of local Washington, DC, housing history.

Introduction

Nearly every discussion of the need to eliminate slum housing in the nineteenth and early twenties centuries included reference to the negative impact of slums on the morality of the inhabitants. There was an oft-spoken and strongly held notion that if poor families were moved from dilapidated to decent, safe, and sanitary housing, their "morals" would improve. The conclusion assumed that because most nonpoor families lived in housing and neighborhoods that were considered decent, safe, and sanitary, and because most nonpoor families adhered to a standard of behavior that was acceptable to their neighbors, uncivil behavior was therefore a natural product of poor housing. Yet there is not, nor has there ever been, any evidence that the mere provision of decent housing impacts the moral or social health of people.

Victorian England

During the Victorian Era in England housing for the poor became a significant social issue. Crammed into neighborhoods that were filled with dilapidated homes, the urban poor were viewed by many outsiders with great misgivings. Writer John Knox wrote of his beloved London, "Surely we mourn that such a city has also much wickedness and profligacy, infidelity, heathanism, and degradation." He urged his readers "to go to the courts and alleys and dens and houses of the poor and see the vast numbers of cringing, shivering, cunning, bigoted, ignorant, selfish, careless, and indifferent creatures who lounge away their Sabbaths and know little besides dirt and degradation." The poverty, dirt, and excess of the slums made the upper classes uncomfortable.[1]

The slums were points of corruption where drunkenness, fighting, and prostitution defined the inhabitants.[2] Their ways seemed almost as disease: contagious and deadly.

The fact that the poor lived in poorly-maintained abodes struck the upper class as the clear cause of their immorality. "If there were no courts and blind alleys, there would be less immorality and physical suffering," wrote Goodwin in 1854. The scourge of poor housing was described as "small in dimensions, and moderate elevation, very closely packed in ill-ventilated streets and courts . . . beyond the congested land around the center, where overcrowding is carried to the greatest success."[3] Slum housing was thought to cause the spread of social disease among inhabitants.

The challenge to the Victorian conception of "home" was an undeniably important factor in the concern of the upper classes to the unsettling crisis.[4]

"Home," in the Victorian sense of the word, embodied religious and familial responsibility. The flawed character of the poor was caused by the corruptive nature of their homes and the improvement of their homes would ultimately improve their moral character.

More important, however, was the feeling that the improvement of slums was uniquely the responsibility of the upper classes. As intellectual and moral superiors in their own minds, it was clear that the socially spirited felt an obligation to pass on their wisdom to their less fortunate brethren.[5] The controlling classes felt that slums and the behavior of those who inhabited them were a disgrace to societies, which considered themselves accomplished and of a high order. That conclusion alone motivated efforts to improve urban housing conditions.

New York Tenements

In the nineteenth and early twentieth centuries, New York City was renowned for its stock of tenement housing. The average tenement consisted of four or five stories, with two or more apartments on each floor. Overcrowding was commonplace. In 1864, the 15,309 tenements in the City of New York were home to 495,692 people.[6] The same year, it was estimated that more than one-fourth of tenement houses were without any form of sewer connection.[7] Even those tenement houses that did have sewer connections were generally serviced by the notorious school sink, which was simply a giant toilet in the back yard of tenements, utilized by all residents. It was not uncommon for the sinks to back up allowing human excrement to sit for weeks on end.[8]

Fire codes for tenement houses were virtually nonexistent. As a result, fires often inflicted serious damage. Though fire escapes were eventually put into a majority of buildings, these ill-conceived structures generally led to central courtyards with no access to the street.

Even fresh air was a commodity in many buildings. Some rooms in tenements had no windows.[9] Overcrowding and stagnant air encouraged the spread of sickness. As a solution to this problem, many tenement houses were eventually equipped with tremendous airshafts running through the center of the building. However, these shafts very often came to be used as garbage receptacles. Some residents threw their refuse into the shafts and thus nullified their function.

Concern grew among public servants and advocates for the poor over the effect of these ghastly conditions on the morality of residents. "Though greatly improved in late years, it [tenement housing] is still the disgrace and curse of the city, that half of the inhabitants live in this class of houses, from which proceeds three-fifths of the crime and three-fourths of the mortality," reported the Asociation for Improving the Condition of the Poor in 1871.[10] Prostitution, murder, and robbery were all too commonly propagated in the slums. The fear of societal contamination once again proved to be a strong influence in the involvement of the upper classes in the lives of the poor.

The New York State Legislature passed laws in 1867, 1879, 1887, and 1895 that required changes in the standards maintained by tenement house landlords.[11] Many advocates for the poor charged landlords with failing to maintain their investments and allowing their tenants to live in filth, which encouraged immoral behavior. However, these laws had little effect on tenement houses.[12] The corruption of the New York City government, combined with the overwhelming number of improvements necessary to bring tenements up to code, made it nearly impossible for basic physical change to occur or for "morals" to improve.[13]

Several charity organizations manifested themselves as a result of government ineptitude. The State Charter Aid Association and the New York Sanitary Reform Society were two of the most notable entities. These organizations primarily encouraged adjustment in the design of tenement houses to create a more healthful, moral atmosphere. Most of these changes, such as the installation of fire escapes and airshafts, failed to produce any tangible improvement in the lives of residents.

After many years of failed efforts to improve housing for the poor in New York City, a housing authority was established in 1934. This action made New York City one of the first jurisdictions in the country to establish a public agency to provide housing for the poor. Its creation spurred later Federal action.

U.S. Federal housing policy for the poor closely followed the general sentiment of historical thought, which dictated that housing conditions influenced social behavior. Few who supported government sponsored housing for low-income families thought that it was important to eliminate the isolation of the poor. In 1909, Frederick Weller, the Director of the Commission on Housing in the Nation's Capital, wrote in his book, *Neglected Neighborhoods*, quoting English sources:

> No improvement in the housing conditions of our town population can have a very large effect in raising the level of civilization and welfare unless it is accompanied by successful efforts to intermix the dwellings of the rich and the poor.[14]

Similar statements were rare, however. More often the emphasis of public policy was the relationship between good housing and high morals.

After it became apparent that the government would become involved in long-term, low-income housing in the 1930s, any thoughts such as those expressed by Weller were admonished by the private housing industry, which feared widespread government involvement in the private market. The concept of public housing was incongruous with the principle of free enterprise. According to the industry, if government became involved in housing, the average landlord would be unable to compete. So to ensure that government would not become enmeshed in the provision of housing, the system was designed exclusively for low-income families who could not afford decent, safe, and sanitary housing.

Though the problems of housing in the late nineteenth and early twentieth centuries in England and the United States were in many ways similar, there was one significant difference. The English learned early on that it was important not to separate the rich from the poor.

Concern over the status of American cities, their unprecedented social problems and fiscal deterioration, has produced many studies and recommendations. This book is concerned primarily with the role of subsidized housing in the decline of many large American cities. Special attention is given to Washington, D.C., in addition to Pittsburgh, Pennsylvania, and Baltimore, Maryland.

The authors believe the social instability that has dominated our cities for many decades has resulted from the following factors:

1. The unprecedented isolation of hundreds of thousands of our poorest and most troubled citizens contributed significantly to the problem;
2. Isolation was the consequence of housing policies and programs that were funded by the Federal government;
3. Urban service institutions, both public and private, were unable to meet the mammoth service requirements of large numbers of isolated, poor families; and
4. Most important, the absence of community to motivate residents to a sense of belonging and control that could lead to shared values.

The reader should note that all italicized parts of this book are firsthand accounts presented by coauthor James G. Banks.

Notes

1. Yelling, J. A., *Slum and Slum Clearance in Victorian England* (London: Birbeck College, University of London, 1986), 16, .
2. Power, N. S. *The Forgotten People, a Challenge to a Caring Community.* (Eversham, England: Arthur James, 1965).
3. *Ibid.*, 20.
4. *Ibid.*
5. Wohl, Anthony S., *The Eternal Slum: Housing and Social Policy in Victorian England.* (Montreal: McGill/Queen's University Press, 1977).
6. Atkins, Gordon. *Health, Housing, and Poverty in New York City: 1865–1898.* (Ph.D. diss., Columbia University, 1947), 55.
7. *Ibid.*, 57.
8. *First Report of the Tenement House Department of the City of New York, 1902–1903* 1: 61.
9. Riis, Jacob A. *The Battle with the Slums.* (1902; Montclair, New Jersey: Patterson Smith, 1969).
10. State of New York Temporary Commission to Examine and Revise Tenement House Law. *Report of Temporary Commission to Examine and Revise the Tenement House Law, State of New York,* 30 January 1928, 9.
11. Veiller, Lawrence, and Robert W. DeForest, *The Tenement House Problem, Including the Report of the New York State Tenement House Commission of 1900. Volume I.* (New York: MacMillan Co., 1903).
12. *Ibid.*
13. Atkins, Gordon, *Health, Housing and Poverty.*
14. Weller, Charles Frederick, *Neglected Neighborhoods,* (Philadelphia: The John C. Winston Company, 1909), 298.

Chapter 1

The Unintended Consequences

The plague of social, cultural and economic problems that has saturated the lives of poor, urban families in the past four decades is the consequence of public policies and programs that separated financially independent families from the poorest, most troubled families.

Characterized by the prevalence of crime, deficient schools, poor health and "questionable morality," areas predominated by the urban poor have been studied extensively to determine the causes of these tragedies. Experts and politicians claiming institutional credibility have undertaken numerous studies and enacted policies both to explain and solve the overwhelming crisis.

Though we pay homage to family and community as the foundations of our civilized society, public responses to social problems that reflect weaknesses in either seem to be restricted primarily to the provision of more money for more physical improvements. If crime increases, more police are needed. If there is recidivism, there must be longer prison terms. It is as though the simplest of equations have been actualized without first determining whether such mechanisms will be of greatest benefit to society.

It is interesting that the best interests of society rarely come into question in general debate over the nature of urban problems. The social framework, which sets the standards for society and limits the possible solutions to urban quandaries, is hardly ever mentioned. Even though human beings created the arrangement of rules and regulations that control the structure of social and economic interaction, somehow, even with the constant ambiguous interpretations of such systemic axioms, we seem to imagine "the system" as immutable.

In the vast majority of urban areas in the United States, there are clear demarcations between rich and poor and between black and white. There is strong evidence that we, as a society, have devised and created environments to isolate the most poor and troubled families in our communities. These environments set in motion a social deterioration that has affected millions of people living in American cities and that has resulted in thousands of untimely deaths, the retardation of the maturation of millions of children, and the diminution of family as a dependable force in human life. These environments have caused the rapid growth of public costs for health programs, the expansion of police forces, court personnel, and, most important, the weakening of the role of black males in their families and communities.

The isolation of the poor has been a fundamental problem of housing policy for many years. Yet there is no evidence that such isolation arose out of hatred for the poor. Rather, this isolation grew out of a genuine interest in helping the financially less fortunate, combined with a misunderstanding about the nature of human growth and development. This confusion has fostered the growth of public and subsidized housing into the focal point of housing for the poor. Whether or not we wish to acknowledge this fact, changes in the admission standards of publicly subsidized housing have greatly impacted the urban environment.

Many studies and reports have emphasized the important role that family and community play in the establishment of a stable and civilized society. Yet, there is no established public policy to protect families or communities from deterioration. The reluctance to establish such policy may stem from a national bias against "social planning." Physical planning is intended to produce tangible results. Social planning typically is not warmly endorsed because the evidence of success is often intangible and requires a long maturation period.

The difficulty of addressing the failure of a system that was created to warehouse the poor is twofold. First, it is readily apparent that critical self-assessment and acceptance of responsibility for failure are not easy tasks for people in general and particularly for those who work with the poor. After all, helping the poor is a symbol of morality. The second complication in addressing the system, which has divided the rich from the poor, is far more serious and daunting. That is, what are the questions that must be asked to begin to change the system, and how will those questions lead to appropriate solutions? If we truly seek equality and righteousness, there is no greater task than to question the system of government housing programs for the poor, which has so severely impacted this country, affecting the health, safety, and welfare of all Americans.

Public Housing

In the early days of public housing, it was clear that the program was intended as a stepping-stone toward independent living. Families in need of support during difficult financial times received aid to meet their housing costs until they achieved economic stability. Housing authorities made significant efforts to ensure that public housing provided opportunities for the pursuit of strong families, good health, and enriching community environments. Though there were misgivings in some areas where public housing was built, the early days of the system did not prove to be terribly disruptive to surrounding communities. Many public housing residents became active in their new neighborhoods and took part in community civic life.

Although public housing was originally specifically for low-income families, since its inception there has been substantial change in the criteria for selecting residents. Following World War II, the structure of urban communities began to change. Housing was built in the suburbs to meet a severe housing shortage and to boost the health of the housing industry. In the process it also encouraged exclusivity for white families who were seeking to escape the growing minority populations in cities. Urban areas became home to an increasing number of poor people, many of them African American. With the elimination of segregation, some nonpoor blacks moved to areas of the city previously all white, often leaving poorer families without strong communities.

Urban Renewal is considered by many to be the beginning of substantive changes in the criteria used for the selection of residents in the public housing program. Urban Renewal funds were authorized to reclaim deteriorated urban areas by acquiring them under the power of eminent domain and selling them to private developers who would build new housing, commercial buildings and, where appropriate, industrial areas. Families displaced from slums that were purchased under the Urban Renewal Program were given priority for admission to public housing.

Higher priority for people displaced by Urban Renewal brought a change in the profile of residents. Initially populated by two-parent working families, over time, public housing became home for many single-parent families whose principal incomes were from welfare. Projects began to crumble. Disorders increased. Stable families with options moved to other areas.

As the poorest and most troubled of our families have been isolated, we have seen clearly the consequences of leaving members of our society unengaged and without the leadership of more stable families. The neighborhood institutions and organizations that were once active in public housing began to disappear as the more stable population left. Our failure to recognize the importance of community as a prerequisite for civility has led to heightened disorder in many of our large, urban centers.

Community

As the poorest and most troubled families gradually found themselves without the support of extended families and communities, they became increasingly disorganized. The many social service organizations for the poor did not recognize the indispensable role of family and community in resolving individual personal problems.

For years now, we have heard discussions about the underclass and welfare families. We have heard of, and perhaps even seen, deteriorating urban areas predominated by impoverished minorities and brimming with hostility and fear. Few observers recognize the profound sense of rejection felt by the isolated poor.

The most striking and perhaps important commonality among this population, besides its uniform poverty, is its uniform skin coloration. African Americans have been concentrated in exceedingly impoverished public and subsidized housing developments since the beginning of the public housing program. In 1937 segregation by race was publicly sanctioned. Most public housing in the early years of the program provided separate developments for black and white residents. As racial segregation was gradually reduced by legislative and court actions, public housing became the home of the poorest and most troubled African-American families. Though housing segregation was officially eliminated more than thirty years ago, housing for poor black families is often segregated.

Efforts to move poor African American families from public housing concentrated in impoverished areas to areas with less concentrated poverty in Chicago, Yonkers, New York, Pittsburgh, and other cities have met with sharp resistance. There continues to be a fear that the "immoral nature" of impoverished minorities will compromise the civility of the middle class and neighborhood culture and thus supplant mainstream values with disorder and disruption. The negative media coverage and statistics of impoverished minority neighborhoods have reinforced the certainty of cultural inferiority in the minds of many middle-class people.

Public sentiment has never been strongly in favor of changing the public housing system. Both liberal and conservative forces have unwittingly combined to maintain isolated impoverished communities. Conservatives have been reluctant to take measures that would infringe on the free market. On the other hand, advocates for the poor continue to claim the need for sustaining low-income housing and services with little understanding that the concentration of the poor and the provision of services combine to thwart the growth of community.

The system of advocacy has played an extremely efficacious role in the development of urban disorder. Although their actions are certainly intended to prevent the poor and most troubled in society from sinking to the depths of financial and social purgatory, their efforts are sometimes self-serving. It sounds rather odd to conceive of an industry devoted to the "less fortunate" as being self-serving. Some might consider such an assessment an oxymoron. Too often success is measured in terms of the number of clients served rather than the reduction of need for the service.

Services

Family and community deterioration has contributed to the shortcomings of public services. Many public services addressed to human needs, from the beginning, were based on the often unspoken yet well understood assumption that stable families and community play a significant role in the success of the service.

Home and community deterioration also contribute to the intensification of the problems of families using other public services. Fear of violence has severely reduced the use of recreation facilities in many poor communities. Welfare workers often find resentful clients and unfriendly neighborhoods; welfare clients often fail to keep appointments because another emergency has demanded their attention. Public health facilities that serve the poor are burdened by misuse.

Resembling intensive care units, neighborhoods that warehouse the urban poor are in a perpetual state of submission. Organizations that claim professional knowledge of problems have the ability to make decisions that, in other communities, would be left to residents. Further impacting the autonomy of people living in these environments is the sheer number of organizations that provide services. For example, in one section of Washington, DC, where there is a great deal of government-sponsored housing, many residents are serviced by between six and sixteen different agencies.

Splintered and uncoordinated, many organizations require residents to accept new rules and schedules. Because public and private agencies often overlap in their goals and compete for the attention of both residents and funders, there is sometimes little motivation to coordinate efforts. Residents rarely seek to challenge decisions made by these organizations.

It is not surprising that as the human service needs of a community grow, the number of organizations and individuals hoping to play a role in serving the poor also grows. Sometimes, there is little attention given to whether or not people want these services. Most of the service givers are convinced that they have the very thing that is needed to correct inadequacies. One after the other, they come offering a sure cure for the patients. Sadly, in spite of the best efforts of some social service agencies, the intensity of the problems remains unabated in many cities.

Out of Control

Anger and sadness of an incalculable depth tear at the souls of people who feel that they are unloved, uncared for, discarded, and forgotten about by society. When entire neighborhoods are made up of people with these feelings of despair, who feel powerless and withdraw from common activities, isolated areas of the poor are left to ruin.

Because of the severe lack of communication within communities of extreme impoverishment, the normal, informal support groups found in most neighborhoods are absent. Leadership and responsibility are scarce. *Informal social control*, a term that refers to the development, observation, and enforcement of norms for appropriate public behavior, helps to maintain order in areas that are not plagued by serious social problems. Neighbors who are estranged from one another and who are constantly under a barrage of problems have little time and little desire to take the steps that are necessary to establish informal social discipline.

The lack of informal social control added to the preponderance of severe problems faced by residents has created an atmosphere in which hostility and mistrust are the norm. Fearful of the anger from others, individuals shy away from correcting misbehavior when it is encountered. To gain respect within their community, young people often find themselves drawn into what some outsiders may find to be antisocial behavior. Dealing drugs, using drugs, committing violence, and promiscuous sex are acts associated with antisocial, urban poor. Residents of impoverished urban areas face the rest of the world, which sees only their weaknesses. As the outside world celebrates a culture based on financial prosperity, cartoon-like violence, and sexual potency, impoverished urbanites attempt to emulate the outside world. The urban poor are constantly seeking a sense of self-worth and respectability. Because the normal channels of expression are closed to them, they use the forbidden ones. They are easy targets for those who control the underground drug market. Their economic instability and their desire to escape their surroundings leads them to take risks with tragic consequences, including injury, disease, incarceration, and premature death.

The New Social Control

Because there is no strong, widely accepted community social control, outside organizations have sought to maintain some sense of order so that the disorganization found in poor urban neighborhoods will not contaminate others. In the past twenty years, enforcement of social standards has been undertaken largely by the police. The calls for tougher sentencing of criminals, increased police presence, and the construction of more jails are primarily for poor, urban offenders. A growing industry has evolved to contain the criminals, who are mostly young, minority males. Billions of dollars are spent every year to try to maintain order. Yet the causes of disorder remain unaddressed.

The desire to punish criminals to the full extent of the law has been perpetrated most often against young African-American men. Recent studies have shown that young black men are arrested at a higher rate, prosecuted at a higher rate, and sent to prison for longer sentences than their white counterparts who commit similar acts. The removal of young men from communities during formative years has a tremendously severe impact upon them. Traditional male-female long-term relationships are inhibited. Job prospects for the incarcerated are extremely limited after release. Male role models are absent, which forces children to establish their own standards.

Children

The greatest tragedy of this environment is its impact upon the young. Single mothers, without the means or the will to support themselves, sometimes use drugs, solicit for prostitution, and suffer from some level of depression. They often find it difficult to meet their parental responsibilities effectively. This neglect not only impacts the individual child, but also those public services that serve the young, such as public schools, the foster care system, and health care.

Public schools originally operated on the assumption that most students would come ready to link formal education to the learning they had experienced with their families and neighbors. More important, children were expected to come to school with behavior patterns that assured that they would respect and obey the teacher and other school employees. Disruptive students were few in number and thus required less attention from teachers. Now we know that if a large proportion of students arrive at school without the learning that home and community are expected to provide, formal education can be significantly obstructed.

Schools located in severely distressed urban areas are forced to deal with problems that are not as extensive in more affluent areas. Hunger, violence, and neglect assume a sense of authority in schools that service severely impoverished children. Most successful schools are those where young people are supported by parents who value education and assume a bright future for their children. Parents and children living in public housing and in impoverished areas, however, often do not always have such a rosy view of the prospects that education can provide. Intellectual stimulation is not an everyday occurrence for many children in impoverished communities. Teachers rarely get a chance to meet the parents of their students. Finding their environment increasingly difficult to deal with, skilled, qualified teachers move on to better schools. Children of parents who are concerned with the quality of education move their children from schools that serve an increasingly poor population and leave a largely dysfunctional school environment.

Children who come from abusive homes, which are unfortunately quite common in poor, urban communities with public housing, often become a part of the foster care system. Increasing cases have added pressure to government agencies that are assigned the job of protecting children in danger. Whereas the need to place children in safe and loving homes has increased, the availability of such homes has not. African-American children from homes in public housing where they have experienced neglect face doubtful odds of being in stable homes for long periods of time. With the lingering effects of abuse, they often face prolonged periods of loneliness and despair precisely when they are in need of the greatest support.

After years of working in neighborhoods of extreme poverty in Washington, D.C., it has become undeniably apparent that our provision of housing for the poor has come at the cost of families and communities. If we truly seek to provide social and economic opportunities for the poor, we must rid our cities of pockets of concentrated poverty.

Chapter 2

Divergent Neighborhoods

During the early decades of the twentieth century, Anacostia, located in Far Southeast Washington, DC was perceived as an undeveloped and a relatively unimportant part of the Nation's Capital. Indeed, in the minds of many Washington residents, Anacostia was a rural area that was struggling to achieve the sophistication associated with life in the Nation's Capital.

Anacostia was separated into four loosely defined subdivisions: Barry Farm, Uniontown, Congress Heights, which was composed primarily of moderate and middle income white families, and Garfield, which was home to low and moderate income black families. This part of Washington, DC, with its rolling hills and lush greenery, has views of two rivers, the Anacostia and Potomac, as well as views of downtown Washington, northern Virginia, and even small parts of Maryland.

To reach Anacostia from the central city it was necessary to travel south on 11th Street, S.E., past the gas plants that produced domestic gas. That route led to the bridge that spanned the Anacostia River.

Barry Farm

The Commission of Refugees, Freedmen, and Abandoned Land was established on 4 March 1865. After the assassination of President Abraham Lincoln, General O. O. Howard was named commissioner of the agency, which came to be informally called The Freedmen's Bureau. In 1867 General Howard created a Board of Directors for the Bureau, which included Senator S. C. Pomeroy of Kansas and John Elvans, a local businessman. Today, streets in Barry Farm bear the names of these two board members. The newly appointed board was authorized to use fifty-two thousand dollars from an educational fund available to the Bureau to acquire land to sell, lease, or rent to free blacks. The authorization included instructions that profits from the sale would be used to provide support for institutions of higher learning established for blacks, including Howard University. The three hundred and seventy-five acres was purchased from the heirs of James D. Barry in 1867 by the Freedmen's Bureau. Freed men were hired at $1.25 a day to fell trees and cut roads through the area to be cleared and settled first. For $125 to $300, a family could purchase a one-acre plot and enough lumber to build a house.[1]

The Bureau's plan to purchase land to sell to free blacks was not well received among the white population. Initial efforts to purchase vacant plots in the vicinity of the Washington Navy Yard were spurned. The Bureau therefore resorted to secret negotiations with the heirs of James Barry to purchase the Barry Farm' of three hundred and seventy-five acres.

As slaves, many of the men who lived in Barry Farm had been trained as carpenters, brick layers, or roofers. These men soon came to know that, together, they could build homes for themselves. The work was hard and because most of the men had other employment, work on homes usually took place after normal work hours and on weekends. The women often brought meals to the work site and even held lanterns as their husbands worked to finish the homes. As each house was completed, the community celebrated with singing and dancing.

Many men living in Barry Farm were regularly employed at St. Elizabeth's Hospital (a mental institution), the Washington Navy Yard, or the local gas plant, all within walking distance of most homes in Anacostia. Because many residents had some building and construction skills, they were also able to obtain periodic employment both locally and elsewhere in the city as handymen. The few residents with college educations were employees of the Federal or local government. Some were school teachers or clerks. Many of the educated residents in the Barry Farm area came from other parts of the city. They had enjoyed the benefits of a higher level of public education from strong churches where special schools had been initiated.

In the early twentieth century, Barry Farm was not serviced by sewers, electricity, or gas. Water was available only from street hydrants. Few streets had electric lighting. Some were serviced by gas lights that were required to be turned up each evening and down each morning, a job typically performed by a local resident. Residents used coal and wood for cooking and heating. Kerosene lamps also provided lighting and heating for homes.

At the turn of the century, my father held two jobs, one at the Washington Navy Yard, the other was with the US Postal Service processing mail. My father was admitted to Howard University Law School. Although he had not attended college, still working two jobs, he received his LLB in 1911. My father's example was an important part of my development.

I was born in Barry Farm in 1920. I think I was lucky to have been raised in Barry Farm, to have known all those people, to have had a family that really believed it could achieve, no matter what the barrier. We seldom discussed racial obstacles; more often we talked about the importance of education and the achievement of a state of independent living.

In the early 1900s, my father purchased two lots in the Barry Farm area: one for himself, the other for my grandfather who had, as a slave, escaped at the age of sixteen from Spotsylvania County, Virginia. He worked for the Bureau of Engraving and Printing. My father had studied mechanical drawing at Armstrong High School. After subsequent employment with a licensed black architect located in Northwest Washington he was able to design houses. With those skills he designed our house, his father's house, and houses for at least six other families in the area. One of the houses is still standing on Elvans Road in Barry Farm.

On each of the lots that my father purchased, they built a two-story frame house. Both included a living room, dining room, kitchen, and pantry, all accessible by means of a hallway on the first floor. On the second floor were three bedrooms and two smaller extra rooms. Our yard, nearly an acre, was planted with flowers, vegetables, and fruit trees. We also had a chicken house and pig pen.

The education and support for their children's spiritual growth and physical well-being was the most important issue for residents of Barry Farm. This included not only formal education in schools, but also that provided by individual residents who shared their skills and special interests with others, particularly children.

At least three neighbors gave piano lessons when I was growing up. Though many of the women were employed, they also assisted in building houses and shared their knowledge about sewing and cooking. Many made clothing for their families. A few acquired sewing machines, which they shared with each other.

The families we knew nurtured the inquisitive nature of children. As a child growing up in the Barry Farm area, I remember the constant emphasis on education and learning. Many parents were eager for their children to overcome racial obstacles by excelling in school. Completing homework assignments was a high priority. A high percentage of the parents maintained contact with teachers by attending Parent-Teacher Association meetings and individual conferences.

Cooking was a frequent topic as neighbors discussed the events of the day. Some mothers were well known for their fried chicken or kidney stew or fried oysters. My mother's most enduring cooking accomplishment was her preparation of hot rolls for Sunday dinner. The process began on Saturday night when she prepared the ingredients, including yeast, to rise for use the next morning. It was not unusual for her to share her recipes with neighbors as her sons bragged about their mother's cooking.

Community forms when people find that they need each other to survive and prosper. People in Barry Farm found common interest in educating their children, getting water and sewer services in the neighborhood, and having the streets paved and then lit with electric lamps. They formed civic organizations to accomplish community goals, met frequently in schools, at PTA meetings, at churches, and at stores, where they began to have some confidence and cohesiveness as a group. The bonds of community became stronger.

Churches and civic associations played a major role in helping migrants from the South to find their way in Anacostia and establish themselves in this new environment. Though current records do not specify the number of migrants from the deep south, there were families from Mississippi, Georgia, North and South Carolina, Tennessee, Alabama, and West Virginia. Many families also came from Maryland and Virginia. The community helped the migrants to find homes and jobs and to connect with the appropriate schools. Most important, they were welcomed and invited to become active in churches and civic groups.

Serving not only as centers for worship, many churches offered cultural opportunities such as concerts, dramas, and, later, movies. Regular church-sponsored social events, primarily dinners, served not only to raise money but also to enrich the relationships between neighbors.

My parents were extremely active participants in church life. We were members of the St. John's Colored Methodist Episcopal (CME) Church. My paternal great grandfather had been the minister there many years before I was born, and most of my family continued as members.

In addition to three regular services on Sunday and prayer meetings on Wednesday, the church sponsored picnics at the National Zoo; bus trips to the beaches of the Chesapeake Bay; piano and violin concerts; and dramatic productions, musicals, and lawn parties. Church membership absorbed most of the free time of members. It encouraged members to commit to help each other wherever needed. Illness and death brought immediate offers of help, donations of cooked meals, care for children, and many hands to help the families cope. In fact, many of the services now offered by charitable agencies came unrequested from neighbors who believed it was their duty, no matter what the sacrifice, to help their neighbors. These activities and the structure were the same in most of the churches in Anacostia.

My father was, for many years, the Superintendent of Sunday school and a member of the Board of Trustees. My mother taught Sunday school but managed to prepare a special after–Sunday school breakfast for her family, featuring her special hot rolls. Father was often the chairperson of Men's Day and Mother was occasionally the chairperson of Women's Day. Both participated in the celebration of Children's Day.

Church sponsored a Sunday evening program called the Epworth League. The League encouraged young members to read books and articles that would broaden our understanding of our country and explore the opportunities offered for growth. We were encouraged to read Booker T. Washington, W. E. B. DuBois, and other well known authors. Occasionally two or more League members were assigned the same book so that the variations in interpretations could be included in the verbal reports. Discussions were often heated. After presentations, there were questions and answers, which often led to agreements to gather more information.

My father was also active in civic life as the Chairman of the Barry Farm Civic Association. Though it met only once each month, the Chairman responded to inquiries from residents almost daily and prepared and offered testimony on community problems to Congressional committees that oversaw the District of Columbia. With these responsibilities came frequent requests to speak to other community groups.

In addition to our schoolwork, my three brothers and I worked around the house doing chores. There were chickens to be fed, wood to be chopped for the kitchen stove, coal buckets to be filled for space heaters, and water to be brought in from the street hydrant. The work was all part of the system of survival. It didn't occur to us that this work was a burden. It had to be done for the good of the family.

In my family there was, from the earliest days of my life, the unchallenged assumption that each of us, the four brothers, would attend college. In addition to our chores, reading newspapers, magazines, and books was a part of each day's activities. When we began school we were not only properly dressed (including neckties), but we were also never late and always completed our homework. There were no excuses and no exceptions. As a result, three of us earned undergraduate and graduate degrees. In some other families in the area, children became medical doctors, lawyers, school teachers, social workers, college professors, military officers, and public officials.

Barry Farm was a village, a community. There were leaders and residents who cared about one another. The contact between neighbors led to a high level of trust and respect and thus to a shared set of values and expectations.

Though not all neighbors were intimate friends, they shared greetings as they met on the street and often inquired about children or family. It was a village where the education of children was assigned high priority and where school teachers were accorded the highest esteem. There is no hiding when people live that close together. As a result, there was limited antisocial behavior.

The positive impact of successful neighbors on others who have not yet reached success can be described as *leaven*. Key to the effectiveness of leaven is a pattern of association between those in need of encouragement and help and those neighbors who can provide help. In a neighborhood where churches, schools, civic groups, and community activities are strong, the effectiveness of leaven is most assured.

Leaven among neighbors is dependent upon how well the "dough" of neighborly relations is kneaded. The more frequent and positive the meetings between neighbors, the stronger the bonds. As in most human ventures, there were a few families who did not benefit from the leaven of the community in Barry Farm. This was principally because they did not join their neighbors in day-to-day community-driven efforts and thus were never enfolded into kneading the system. Because most residents were a part of the process, the leaven in Barry Farms produced a community with a united spirit of confidence.

Southwest

At the same time that Barry Farm became home to hundreds of freed slaves and their families, the Southwest section of the Nation's Capital struggled to provide housing for thousands of freedmen as well..[2]

Southwest was composed of large blocks of row houses with considerable space between them in the rear. These areas were essentially alleys. These alleys soon evolved into inexpensive housing developments for Freedmen. In a short period of time, large numbers of alley dwellings were built. Southwest was more developed than rural Anacostia at that time.

The alley dwellings were built primarily in the blocks that were occupied by black families. By 1871, the city directory reported fifteen hundred households in just one hundred and eighteen alleys. Eighty-one percent of alley dwellers were black and largely unskilled service workers. By 1897, the city's alley population numbered 17,244 or eleven percent of the total city population, living in two hundred and thirty-seven blocks. Black residents constituted ninety-three percent of the alley population.[3] Employers appreciated having the alley dwellings in Southwest as it was easier for employees to get to work. The management of several warehouses that were located in that area wanted their employees to live nearby.

The houses had two stories, with two rooms per floor. They had outside toilets and outside spigots for water. There was no electricity and no gas. Residents were plagued by overcrowding, frequent fires, and inadequate sewage disposal. These conditions had a significant impact on the health of the residents. The death rate of alley dwellers was twice that of street dwellers. For the younger residents, death was even more common. One-third of all babies born to mothers living in alleys died before the age of three.[4]

Although many acknowledged the severe health problems of alley dwellers, of greater concern to the community at large was the plague of immorality that came to characterize life in the alleys. Rape, robbery, and murder were more common in the world hidden from the street. It was as though the alley dwellings possessed their own culture and set of standards that were entirely different from those of the rest of the citizens of the city. There were quite a number of alley dwellings in other sections of the city besides Southwest, but they were more scattered. Southwest was the smallest quadrant in the city but contained most of the alley dwellings. Its reputation for immorality was derived from these alleys.

"Laws that are necessary for the general public health and public welfare of a community hardly work for the poor," complained Frederick Siddons in testimony before Congress on the matter of Alley Dwellings. He continued,

> Living in these narrow crowded interior courts and alleys always produce evil conditions.... I think it is only human that we accustom ourselves to condition of life and living. If the surroundings are demoralizing, people steadily degenerate under those demoralizing conditions.[5]

In addition to the people living in alleys, there was a section of Southwest close to the railroad tracks that had been taken over by people who, today, might be called homeless. They were not regular residents anywhere. They sometimes slept on the street but often found temporary shelter with friends who lived in the alleys.

Charitable organizations that were created to solve the alley dwelling issue did little to solve the problem. The Washington Sanitary Improvement Company rebuilt alley dwellings on a large scale to meet the same standards as mainstream homes. The Washington Sanitary Housing Company built new homes for alley dwellers. Yet these efforts had little impact upon the problems associated with alley dwellings.

The alley dwellers of Southwest were in a completely different environment from the people that I knew growing up in Barry Farm. Southwest was a fractured neighborhood. The people who faced the street, both black and white, did not welcome the alley dwellers whom they believed had no vested interest in the area. The alley dwellers spoke with thick accents and had country ways. They were generally poorer and less educated. Many alley dwellers felt rejected by their neighbors whose homes faced the street. Southwest residents who faced the street had established their community and its institutions long before the recently freed slaves had begun to migrate. The newcomers were seen as intruders, without the potential to become good neighbors.

The houses that faced the interior of the block were clear examples of rejection. Back yards were places for people and things that one wished to conceal. Of course, not everyone or even most people living in alleys participated in "morally reprehensible" activities. The alleys, however, were characterized as such because of this fractured neighborhood of immigrants. The alley dwellers were pariahs who were unwanted by the families who enjoyed the respectability of living in houses that faced the street. Few of the existing civic institutions and churches welcomed the alley dwellers.

The residents of alley dwellings in Southwest were not forced to rely on one another. They moved into houses that were already built and worked at factories owned by people who were already established in the city. In Barry Farm, people had to do for themselves.

Barry Farm and Southwest areas serve as clear examples of the role that strong community and families must play in developing a neighborhood that is civil and stable. That the Barry Farms residents were responsible for the total development of the area is crucial to understanding its stability. The residents came there with very little and planned and built their own housing and started businesses. The families that went to Southwest found housing already built and no opportunity to own businesses themselves. The employment that was available to them was almost exclusively for unskilled laborers. Furthermore, they were not encouraged or invited to participate in the affairs of the community where they lived or to attend its churches. From the beginning, they were outcasts.

Notes

1. Hutchinson, Louise Daniel, *The Anacostia Story, 1609–1930,* (Washington, DC: Smithsonian Institution Press, 1977), 82–83.
2. Kober, George M., *The History of the Housing Movement in the City of Washington, DC* (Washington, DC: Washington Sanitary Housing Companies, 1925), 2.
3. James Borchet, *Alley Life in Washington, DC* (Washington, DC: Proceeds of the Washington Historical Society, 1980.
4. Senate Committee on the District of Columbia, *Discontinuance of Alley Dwellings in the District of Columbia: Hearings on S. 2675,* 77th Congress, 2nd Sess., 1922, pp. 3-54
5. Subcommittee of the Committee on the District of Columbia, Inhabited Alleys of the District of Columbia and Housing Unskilled Workingmen: Hearings on S. 1624, 2376, 2397, 2589, 4592, and 4672, 63rd Congress, 2nd Sess., 1914, pp. 7, 12.

Chapter 3

The Creation of Public Housing

The Federal Government was extremely active in its attempts to resolve the problems of the Depression. In particular, new programs that were created to prevent the foreclosure and loss of housing gave much needed aid to both mortgage lending institutions and private citizens. The Federal Home Loan Bank was created in 1932 to act as a reserve system to provide stability to savings and loan associations, savings banks, and thrift institutions. Widespread default on loans, prior to Federal aid, had resulted in a diminished level of confidence among real estate investors and lending institutions. The Federal Home Loan Bank lowered the level of risk for financial institutions that made mortgage loans to private citizens. For many mortgage lenders, this restored some confidence.[1]

The Federal Housing Administration (FHA) was perhaps the most influential institution created in the difficult Depression era. The FHA actively transformed the mortgage system by reducing down payments, and providing long-term mortgages, reduced monthly payments, and reduced interest rates. These changes were meant to encourage homeownership among people who, previously, would not have been able to purchase their own homes. Even today the FHA is one of the most widely known and used of all government housing programs. Finally, the Home Owners Loan Corporation provided financial aid to homeowners in danger of losing their homes for failure to make mortgage payments.[2] As a whole, however, these efforts did not address the large, desperate population that rented. Homeownership was an unrealistic hope for millions of renters who continued to call substandard housing "home."

An estimated forty million people were without adequate housing. As a result, the Public Works Administration (PWA) undertook the construction and management of a limited number of housing projects to meet some of the extensive housing need.The housing department of the PWA built and managed fifty-one projects during the three-and-a-half-year period of its existence (though these projects came under the rule of housing authorities). Its limited scope afforded but little aid to the millions of people who were plagued by the Depression. Yet the mere presence of the housing department of the PWA, as well as the presence of other government housing-related programs, signaled a new tolerance for government efforts to improve housing for the poor.

The Housing Act of 1937

It became substantially apparent that the efforts to stem the massive economic problems of the nation and provide housing for its poor population were not entirely effective. As the Depression continued to wreak havoc, the search for innovative strategies for relief of the housing problem became even more heated.

In Europe, the inability of the private housing market to assume responsibility for housing the poorest in society had precipitated a stirring government response. Long-term government-sponsored programs, created to ensure that all in society had a decent place to live, had been developed in countries such as Belgium, England, and Italy even before the world financial crisis. These programs provided inspiration for policy-makers in the United States who sought inventive yet realistic strategies to combat the perils of the Depression.

Beginning in the mid-1930s, serious consideration of long-term housing sponsored by the Federal government made its way into social and political circles. Many advocates for public housing felt that the private housing market would never be able fully to provide for the poor and that there was a strong need for Federal government intervention. There was a clear feeling among early public housing advocates that a government-run housing program would be more attentive and supportive of the efforts of residents to shed the shackles of dependency than were the unsympathetic private market. The widespread impact of slum areas all across the country upon the fiscal health of metropolitan areas provided great incentive for an innovative strategy. Traditional municipal services were being drained by the proliferation of problems in slum areas. For example, in Cleveland, Ohio, slum areas accounted for a mere 2.5 percent of the population and yet twenty-one percent of all murders. In Louisville, Kentucky, crime was 4.6 times higher in slum areas than in other neighborhoods.

In many cities, slum areas also were responsible for significantly higher levels of disease. Police, fire, and health services were monopolized by low-income areas. Many cities spent between four, and five times as much money on citizens who lived in slum communities as they did for citizens living in other parts of the city.[4]

"The cost of slums, in terms of dollars and cents results in too great a drain upon the public treasury to continue," said Secretary of the Interior Harold Ickes in Hearings before the Committee on Education and Labor of the United States Senate in testimony before the Senate Education and Labor Committee in 1936[5]. In that year, the first attempt to pass legislation to create a federally sponsored housing program was undertaken. Senator Robert Wagner from New York was the strongest proponent of this legislation. Devoted to his home state, Wagner recognized the urgent need to develop an innovative, long-term strategy to improve the lives of slum dwellers. Yet the passage of the Housing Act of 1936 was not to be.

Although there was strong sentiment among public servants, clergymen, and citizens about the need for a new, innovative strategy, to stem the tide of urban decay and provide financial relief during the Depression, there was an equally loud and powerful interest group of people who were wary of government-sponsored housing. Though they had provided no evidence of success in changing the national predicament, the private housing industry strongly opposed government efforts to become involved in this most lucrative business. The National Association of Real Estate Boards (NAREB) was the most notable and perhaps vocal private housing industry opponent of government attempts to establish a public housing program.

The concern of the private housing industry over Federal involvement in the housing crisis stemmed from a high level of distress over the seeming disregard for free market practices that served the nonpoor. Real estate, though less so during the Depression, was still a valuable commodity. According to private housing advocates, impingement upon any sector of the housing market by government was seen as threatening the ability of the housing industry as it sought to retain control over the well established, free-market system.

However, the actions and speech of government officials and advocates for the poor never signaled that the desired housing program would include provisions for the nonpoor.[6] There was a strong conviction that the physically degenerative environments had an equally socially degenerative impact upon the poor. All previous plans, including those of charitable organizations, addressed the provision of physical change. Slum clearance, reconstruction, and the development of housing became the primary focus of Federal legislation and followed the lead of cities such as New York and Washington, DC.

Testimony before the Congressional committee gave assurances that public housing would not compete with the private market.[7] Income ceilings, to keep out those who might deprive a poor family of a home, were deemed necessary. Limitations on the amenities included in public housing were unquestionably needed to keep down costs and make it less competitive.[8] By restricting the architectural design and incomes of residents of public housing, legislators assured the private housing industry of its continued stronghold. Public housing was not seen as suitable for middle-class neighborhoods. It would remain, generally, in poor communities. The program also provided additional opportunities for employment, which were considered essential by all parties.

After much debate, the Housing Act of 1937 passed. The Act established the United States Housing Authority, a body with power to distribute funds to approved housing authorities in areas that could document a need for public housing. Local housing authorities were given the ability to construct and maintain facilities and to oversee the admission of applicants. With this bill, housing advocates for the poor were confident that a long-range commitment to the preservation of low-income housing was in place. The private housing industry, on the other hand, won assurance that only those people without the means to live in their housing would have the ability to live in the government-sponsored homes.

Residents of Public Housing

In 1937, racial segregation was accepted throughout the country, creating separate white and "Negro" public housing projects. Indeed, whites were a significant majority (seventy to seventy-five percent) of the public housing population for the first two decades of the system

Approximately three-quarters of all residents who entered public housing during the 1940s moved from "substandard" housing conditions.[10] The term "substandard" generally referred to conditions of overcrowding, disrepair, faulty plumbing or lack thereof, and uncleanness. Though it offered low rents, the move to public housing did not necessarily mean a reduction in rent for tenants. Nearly one-third of tenants coming into public housing during the early years of its existence actually paid more for rent than they had paid for their previous housing.[11]

Although the public housing legislation stipulated a certain level of rent subsidy, it is important to remember that the basic operating costs, in the first few decades of public housing were covered by the rents paid by tenants. To generate the required revenue, it was important for housing authorities to admit residents with incomes at a high enough level to insure that rents would meet operating expenses. Consequently, the vast majority of families living in, and moving into, public housing had at least one working member. Families who received public assistance as their primary income were generally restricted to a much lower percentage of residents.

Cohabitation between the sexes, without formal ties, and unwed motherhood were not accepted. Most single parent families were the result of death or work displacement. Annual reports of local housing authorities from the first decade of the public housing program rarely mention the proliferation of single-parent families precisely because they were not a significant portion of residents.

The population of public housing was not the only element of the system that differed from current images. The commitment of local housing authority personnel to ensure the prosperity of their tenants was significantly different. Public housing was not considered a catch-all. It was not a safety net exclusively for the destitute. Authorities held to strict standards by which they judged applicants for admission. Employees of housing authorities often met potential residents in their homes to ensure that they were responsible parents and neighbors. The atmosphere was one of mission and caring, but one that encouraged self-reliance and urged residents to take initiative in the rehabilitation of their lives.

Some housing authorities, mindful of the need to demonstrate the benefits of public housing, kept abreast with positive changes through special studies and detailed records of resident experiences. For example, the annual report of the Housing Authority of Baltimore, Maryland, reported that a municipal study showed that whereas the juvenile delinquency rate of children city-wide was 22.6 per thousand, for children living in public housing, the rate was 13.4 per thousand. The incidence of tuberculosis for the city was 29.7 per 10,000 and in public housing the incidence was 18.6. These figures were offered to document that public housing residents were less often the source of delinquency and the victims of tuberculosis than the average throughout the city.

The Housing Authority of Philadelphia, Pennsylvania reported in 1943 that the average resident of public housing moved to "homes of their own" (owner occupied) after a stay of only five years in public housing. The city also reported that the rates for tuberculosis and pneumonia were higher in the general population of the city than for residents of public housing. The same held true for criminal offenses and juvenile delinquency. Clearly these reports indicate significant health and behavior differences between public housing and the rest of the city.

Social Programs

The social programs available in the early days of public housing were typical of what might be found in any other neighborhood at the time. These were not programs merely for entertainment, but to build a foundation for future successful, productive citizens.

The 1944 Newark, New Jersey Housing Authority Annual Report stated,

> More different activities are found in a public housing project than at Madison Square Garden. Groups of all ages use the community halls and meeting rooms for dances, concerts, song fests, amateur shows, movies, handcraft, publishing, nursing, first aid classes, and almost anything else you can think of. There are baby keep-well stations, health clinics, and branches of the public library.

Practical classes were offered to broaden the knowledge base of residents.

The Philadelphia, Pennsylvania Housing Authority reported in its special twenty year summary of public housing that "specialized activities were provided by various public and voluntary agencies at most community centers on public housing developments," including The Philadelphia Department of Recreation, The Philadelphia Department of Public Health, The Philadelphia Board of Education, The Free Library of Philadelphia, Crime Prevention Association of Philadelphia, Young Women's Christian Association, Pennsylvania State University, U.S. Department of Agriculture, Philadelphia County Agricultural Extension Service, Methodist Deaconess Home, Bible Club Movement, Philadelphia Council of the Boy Scouts of America, Girl Scouts of Philadelphia, American Red Cross, Maternal and Child Health Conferences, two kindergartens, two day care centers for children of working mothers, 4-H Clubs, Leadership training for Scout Leaders, and a Home Nursing Class.

Annual reports are customarily self-congratulatory, and there is no reason to suppose that those of housing authorities are any different. However, there is no reason to doubt the general veracity of the reports. For the first few decades of the recorded activities involving residents of housing, it seems clear that the Authorities sought to help residents create a community, often facilitated by programs that emphasized the growth of children. The programs offered to residents were certainly important to maintaining a reasonably cohesive community. But perhaps more importantly was the level of communication between residents that inspired a high level of control.

The activities sponsored and encouraged by housing authorities allowed both parents and children to become involved in community life. In that way, neighbors and their children would get to know one another. Shared experiences and stories helped to invoke a neighborly atmosphere in public housing.

The development of cooperative understanding between neighbors was fundamentally important for the creation and maintenance of social order. The responsibilities associated with living independently were well understood by most families as a result of communication. Being a good neighbor meant keeping your apartment clean, looking out for the children of others, and contributing to voluntary community projects. Young people were generally expected to show the same respect for their neighbors as they would to their parents. If they misbehaved, and such action was witnessed by an adult, their parents were almost certain to hear about it. These were then neighborly duties associated with any community. If residents were unable to live up to official standards of community expectations, steps were taken to correct the situation. In some instances, residents were evicted for failing to maintain important requirements for continued occupancy.

Mangers of public housing projects lived on site during the early days of the public housing program. Residents in need of assistance had at their disposal a direct link to the main office of the public housing authority. Some managers were known to make daily walking inspections of their projects to check on the upkeep and maintenance of the community and to say "good morning" to their neighbors.

This is not to paint an idyllic picture of life in public housing, for there was poverty, and there were some residents who lived in communities but did not come to participate fully in them. However, in general, there was a striking, community-oriented atmosphere that permeated public housing projects in the 1930s and 1940s.

Notes

1. Mason, Joseph, *History of Housing in the US, 1930–1980* (Houston, Texas: Gulf Publishing Company, 1982), 11.
2. *Ibid.*, 10.
3. *US Housing Act of 1936*, Committee on Education and Labor, (Washington, DC: GPO, 1936), pp. 56, 66. 440, Washington, DC GPO, 1936.
4. *US Housing Act of 1936*, Committee on Education and Labor, (Washington, DC: GPO, 1936), 40.
5. *US Housing Act of 1936*, Committee on Education and Labor (Washington, DC: GPO, 1936), pp. 26.
6. *Ibid.,* 56, 66.
7. *Ibid.,* 56, 66.
8. Public Housing Administration, *Residents of Public Housing. Families in Low-Rent Projects: Statistics on Low-Rent Public Housing 1946–1964* (Washington, DC: Public Housing Administration, Statistics Branch).
9. *Ibid.*
10. United States Housing Authority, Statistics Branch, *Families Moving into U.S. Housing Act Developments, 1947–1949.*
11. ———. *Families Moving into U.S. Housing Act Developments, 1947–1952.*

Chapter 4

Early Public Housing in Washington, DC

When the stock market crashed in 1929, I was nine years old. Washington, DC, was in a unique position, even though the rates of poverty during the Depression were the highest for this country in the twentieth century.[1] Because of the presence of the Federal government, the impact of the Depression in Washington, DC, was not as great as it was in other cities. Even so there were several Public Works Administration (PWA) projects that supplemented Washington area joblessness.

Temporary employees and those who worked in retail establishments were affected the most in Anacostia. As a result, some homeowners couldn't pay their real estate taxes and, therefore, lost their houses. Those families moved to whatever rental housing was available at that time. One of our neighbors bought ten or twenty houses over the years and rented them out. But that was rare in Anacostia. Most houses were owned, and there were no apartments.

By the early 1930s our house was serviced by water and electricity, which made a huge difference in lifestyle. By that time we had bought several electric appliances. There was talk in our house about the impact that the Depression was having on the country. We read about it in the newspaper and heard about it on the radio, but we never experienced any difficulties.

I graduated from high school in 1936 and began my college career at Howard University. Whereas my life in Anacostia was hardly affected by the Depression, the same cannot be said for people who lived in alley dwellings in Southwest Washington. The workers in nearby warehouses and businesses located in Southwest were severely affected by the Depression. Unemployment was certainly more common in that area of the city.

The Alley Dwelling Authority

In 1934, the US Congress enacted legislation to address the alley problem in the Nation's Capital. First Lady Eleanor Roosevelt became involved in efforts to improve housing in the Nation's Capital immediately after her husband became President. She became a supporter of the Washington Housing Association, a private, not-for-profit housing advocacy group. For years the Association had sought federal assistance in improving conditions in the city's infamous alleys. Legislation establishing the The Alley Dwelling Authority, which was intended to combat problems with the alleys, was enacted with Mrs. Roosevelt's support. The Alley Dwelling Authority of Washington, DC, (which later became the Housing Authority) was responsible for building a new house facing the street for each alley dwelling demolished. Residents of the alley dwellings were given first priority to live in this public housing.

When World War II began in 1941, and the US government needed workers to support the war effort, many people moved to Washington, DC. The housing stock in the city, however, was not sufficient to meet the population increase.

The Federal government saw the need to build what they called *war housing*, or homes specifically for war workers. The war housing was in several sections of the city, including the Far Southeast area, and more particularly, the Barry Farm community. Soon the Anacostia area had more temporary housing than any other area in Washington, DC.

Working in Public Housing

In 1944, while employed as a machinist at the Washington Navy Yard, working the 4:00 P.M. to midnight shift, I enrolled at the Howard University School of Social Work. I did this under the influence of my professor and friend, sociologist E. Franklin Frazier.

Frazier started the School of Social Work at Howard University. He encouraged me to become a social worker.

Frazier led me to conclude that I could help people to rid themselves of the burden of being a burden. He was adamant in his belief that poverty could only be eliminated if the unemployed were trained and job opportunities were provided. He was impatient with efforts to make the poor comfortable.

My first practicum assignment at the School of Social Work was at the city's Department of Welfare. After one quarter, I told my advisor that working in the Welfare Department was not what I wanted to do.

Welfare did not have a strong, well-conceived objective of helping families to be self-sufficient. I believed that there could be no real comfort for the poor until they became independent. So my advisor referred me to a new assignment at the Housing Authority, which I accepted. After I had been there for three months, I was hired as a full-time interviewer of housing applicants.

The housing authority office located on L Street, N.W., just off of Connecticut Avenue, was not a convenient location for most people who were applying for public housing. Nonetheless, the waiting room was usually full. Some candidates were waiting at the door when the office opened at 9 A.M. Though there were times when people waited for more than an hour for interviews, most were seen within a short time of their arrival.

In the early days of public housing, selection for admission was something for which people competed. Families who were selected realized that they had been given a special privilege. My job was to interview families who were applying for either existing housing or new public housing.

The application for admission required a listing of all family members by age and gender, place of employment, and wages. If income was not from employment, but from public welfare, that, too was recorded. Before the interview was concluded, the interviewer made an appointment to visit the home of the applicant. The purpose of the visit was to observe physical conditions, housekeeping habits, and relations between family members, particularly between parents and children. Interviewers were required to confirm that couples were legally married by requiring applicants to produce certified marriage licenses. Cohabitation between the sexes, without formal ties, and unwed motherhood were not accepted. Most single-parent families were the result of death or work displacement.

After the initial interview and before the home visit, I was required to order a credit Social Service Exchange report for each applicant. I prepared a comprehensive report, which included a profile of the family that summarized all of the information received. The report was submitted to the tenant selection committee, which comprised Housing Authority officials.

It was the general policy of the Housing Authority that families who were dependent on public welfare would not exceed five percent of the total residents. Though the executive director fought strenuously to require a payment of rent covering full operating expenses by welfare clients, that was not approved. Hence, welfare clients paid minimum rents. Because the Housing Authority was required to meet all operating expenses with tenant rents, it was critically important that the residents have average incomes to enable them to pay rents that were equal to the estimated operating expenses. This requirement was the primary reason for restricting the number of welfare families in public housing. There was a less-often expressed, general agreement that residents of public housing should not be the poorest of the poor. Public housing supporters agreed that neighborhoods created under the public housing program should be "normal." Large concentrations of low-income families were not normal. Consequently, the vast majority of families living in and moving into public housing had at least one working member.

My most challenging job as an interviewer was to select all tenants for the newly built Lincoln Heights Public Housing Project. After I had selected the families, I met them at the development to show them their units and introduce them to the manager.

Out of 100 people interviewed, there would be twenty that were not accepted. All families that moved into public housing had some kind of problems. They didn't have to be perfect. But they had to have some stability and give some evidence that they would help to continue a stable environment in the development to which they were going. Our goal was to avoid was people who might be disruptive.

My second job at the housing authority was as a tenant counselor, helping families who were having social or economic difficulties. One of my responsibilities was to determine what services were available to the families who were in need. I became acquainted with most of the publicly and privately sponsored social agencies in the city and was able to refer most of the families who had needs to service centers where they could get help.

Drugs were not a problem in the 1940s. There were some cases of physical abuse, which I referred to agencies that had been established to handle that kind of problem.

There were some families for whom I had to provide the counseling. For example, I'd go and sit and talk with a husband and wife who was having difficulty paying their bills because one or the other wasn't being as prudent as they needed to be. I would suggest that they develop and agree on a budget and that they not violate the budget except with the consent of the other.

Life in War Housing

While I was employed at the Washington Navy Yard as a war worker and assigned for the Housing Authority for my social work practicum, I moved into the Barry Farm War Housing Project with my wife and son. The neighborhood was made up of people who were fairly well employed and aspiring for greater things. Most of the people who lived in the Barry Farm project were not from Washington. The families were from the eastern part of the country, Maryland, Virginia, Pennsylvania, North Carolina, and South Carolina. There were a few, like my family, from Washington, but most of them were from outside of the city. They were pretty well settled by the time I got there in 1945. The families were generally two-parent, working families. I was the head of my family and I was twenty-four years, but I think most of the people were aged thirty or more. Most of the residents at Barry Farm worked in offices or as building attendants, janitors, or guards. There were not too many highly skilled people.

The Barry Farm project was made up of row houses and constructed of concrete block. There were no basements. Each home had a little grass in the back and a little grass in the front, and everybody took care of their own yards. The housing authority furnished lawnmowers so that tenants could cut their own grass. Many residents also planted flowers. It was what you might expect and find in any privately or publicly owned development in those days.

The building where the rent was collected included rooms that the residents could use for parties and various activities. In those days, the activities for children included Boy Scouts and Girl Scouts. Residents of the development volunteered and ran the activities. Residents also used the social rooms for meetings of the tenant association and to hear speakers from the District government talking about plans for changes in the road system or new traffic lights. There were also many social activities. Occasionally they had a dance. The children would often go there to play games, checkers and dominoes, that kind of thing.

We had tennis courts, which were right outside our door, and we had a ball field. There were plenty of places for children to roller skate. The social programs available in the early days of public housing were typical of what might be found in any other neighborhood at the time.

The Status of Public Housing

The Housing Authority's board of directors was essentially a group of noted public officials. The Chair of the Housing Authority was the Chairman of the Board of Commissioners of the District of Columbia, which was the governing body of the city. The District of Columbia at that time was governed by a three-member Commission that was appointed by the president.

The Housing Authority was very highly regarded in the city. The residents of public housing enjoyed the same quality of public services as the people in other privately owned developments. On the other hand, the people living in alleys in Southwest did not get the same kind of services. That was not an official policy, but it certainly was the truth.

Most housing managers lived on the developments. I remember that there was a fellow who was the manager of two developments, Frederick Douglass and Stanton Dwellings. He would get up every morning and inspect the whole development. If he saw any trash anywhere and it happened to have somebody's name on it, he would go to the family and tell them he found trash in the alley. But he didn't do it in an unfriendly way. He was trying to keep the development clean. He wanted residents to live in an environment with order and stability.

Changes in Anacostia

When World War II ended, the population growth in Washington DC that had accompanied the war diminished, but the growth of the city did not. The nation and its capital city faced severe shortages again. With help from the U.S. Government, private developers were able to build new, privately owned apartments with little risk to their own funds. The entire cost of purchasing the property and construction was subsidized by the federal government.

In the late 1940s, white families were not leaving Anacostia. Much of the housing, particularly in the Congress Heights area (also part of Southeast Washington), were apartments that were built for whites. Adjoining Barry Farm there were some apartments built within a two-minute walk of my house for white families. In the Garfield area, which was essentially a black area along the Suitland Parkway, there were a number of apartments built for white families.

Anacostia was seen as an attractive place to develop housing because of its considerable cheap, vacant land, and beautiful views of the city. In support of efforts to provide more housing, the Barry Farms area was zoned R5A, which prohibited the construction of anything but garden-type apartments.

The population increased considerably during the period of building in Anacostia.

In about three decades, Far Southeast became essentially a rental area. In addition to the mostly garden-style apartment private housing, much of the war housing in the city was converted to public housing for low-income families. The war changed the housing stock and the population of many parts of the city, particularly Far Southeast. Soon after, Southwest was to go through changes of its own.

Notes

1. Population Reference Bureau, *A New Look at Poverty in America.* (Washington, DC: Population Reference Bureau, 1998).

Chapter 5

Postwar Housing

The postwar era witnessed a growing call for urban revitalization.[1] Many cities still had downtown areas with vast numbers of abandoned buildings. Substandard housing was widespread, and social problems continued. In 1946, President Harry S. Truman began an effort to gain support for the initiation of an "urban renewal" program to alleviate the plight of the poor and bring cities to a revered status. The National Association of Real Estate Boards (NAREB), an organization that had strongly opposed the establishment of the public housing program in 1937, was intrigued by the notion of government aid to revitalize deteriorating areas. Urban Renewal promised to help private industry, poor families, and municipal governments attain economic and social stability.

The Rise of Urban Renewal

By the late 1940s, the call for an urban renewal program had gained the support of many factions. The Housing Act of 1949 approved the program and established a far-reaching effort to rebuild the troubled cities of America. Slums would be destroyed and replaced with new, modern examples of Americana, according to the supporters of the Act. Simple rebuilding was not the ultimate goal of the program, however. The purpose of Urban Renewal was seen as a part of a national effort to provide a "safe home and decent living environment" for every person living in the United States.[2] Such a task was neither simple nor inexpensive. Urban Renewal was by far the most ambitious municipal program initiated by the federal government.

The revitalization of urban areas raised the problem of the displacement of people and businesses. A significant portion of the people who would be displaced by Urban Renewal did not have the income to afford private housing and therefore were given priority for public housing. The legislation that authorized Urban Renewal created new standards of admission to public housing.[3]

One billion dollars was allocated for slum clearance.[4] About $1.5 billion worth of loans were allocated for the creation of new public housing projects. An unprecedented 810,000 new units were sought over a six-year period. Advocates for the poor flocked to support the legislation, which gave high priority to public housing for families displaced by urban renewal.

With the beginning of the Korean War, however, came a significant reduction in the funds allocated for public housing. President Truman continued to prescribe more housing for war workers but little for the poor.[5] Once again, a war had contributed to a change, albeit necessary, in the focus of public housing.

Over the next decade, barely one quarter of the public housing promised by the Housing Act of 1949 was built. No more than ninety thousand units had been constructed in a single year. More important, however, the changes in admission to public housing were slowly taking hold and influencing the resident population. The population trend prior to the Housing Act of 1949 had been of working, white families, coming from substandard housing. After the Act, things began to change.

Public Housing Statistics

Approximately half of all families that were admitted to public housing during the 1950s were minorities.[6] In large respect, this trend was due to the displacement of minorities by Urban Renewal. But it can also be attributed to the growing general population of minorities in cities.

Table 1. Trend in Percentage of Single-parent Families in Public Housing

Year	% Single-parent Families
1950	22[a]
1952	26[b]
1958	28[c]

(a) *Families Moving into Low Rent Public Housing*, Statistics Branch, Public Housing Administration, Washington, DC, 1950.

(b) *Families Moving into Low Rent Public Housing*, Statistics Branch, Public Housing Administration, Washington, DC, 1952.

(c) *Families Moving into Low Rent Public Housing*, Statistics Branch, Public Housing Administration, Washington, DC, 1958.

Table 2. Percentage of Families in Public Housing Who Came From Substandard Housing

Year	% from Substandard Housing[a]
1950	73
1952	69
1958	60

a. Families Moving into Low Rent Public Housing from the mid 1950s, Statistics Branch Public Housing Administration, 1950, 1952, 1958..

Warnings Against Concentrated Poverty

Very soon after the enactment of the Housing Act of 1949, those who were responsible for administering the public housing program at the city level had serious concerns about both the design of the program and the isolation of poor families.

Testimony before the Subcommittee on Housing of the Committee on Banking and Currency of the US House of Representatives is particularly revealing. Walter E. Alessandroni, executive director of the Philadelphia Housing Authority, is quoted as saying,

> The Philadelphia Housing Authority is particularly interested along with interested civic groups in designing small rows or groups of fairly typical homes at a minimum cost to fit into older but stable neighborhoods. These dwellings would be non-project in nature. However, such a program of scattered construction, which would meet with wide community support is not in accordance with the standards for design regulations of the Public Housing Administration for the construction of projects.[7]

Before the same committee, Lt. General William B. Kean, E.D., of the Chicago Housing Authority, stated,

In large part, the Chicago Housing Authority has built its public housing projects in aid of the clearance of slum areas. The cost of acquiring and clearing slum property has constituted a substantial proportion of total development costs. These costs have determined the type of dwellings which the Chicago Housing Authority has been able to build . . . . We have been forced to build high use projects in the slum areas which we have cleared.[8]

With the desire to provide the best living conditions for low-income families with many children, the Authority wanted to build row houses or walk-up structures.

On 13 February 1956, Ernest J. Bohn, executive director of the Cleveland Metropolitan Housing Authority, is quoted as follows

Due to unrealistic income limitation we have in Cleveland . . . about fifty percent of the families living in public housing—on some form of public assistance—but I submit that when you have as many as fifty-nine percent of your population in public housing estates comprised of broken families—this is not a normal community.[9]

Notes

1. Mitchell, J. Paul, ed., *Federal Housing Policy and Programs: Past and Present* (New Brunswick, New Jersey: Center for Urban Policy Research, 1985), 254.

2. *Housing Act of 1949*, 81st Congress, 1st Session, Senate Committee on Banking and Currency. 1949, p. 3.

3. Hays, R. Allen, *The Federal Government and Urban Housing: Ideology and Change in Public Policy* (Albany: State University of New York Press, 1985), 13–14.

4. *Mason, Joseph B., History of Housing in the US, 1930–1980* (Houston, Texas: Gulf Publishing Company, 1982), 53.

5. Hays, *The Federal Government and Urban Housing*, p. 45.

6. *Families Moving into Low Rent Public Housing* Statistics Branch, Public Housing Administration Washington, DC 1950, 1952, 1958.

7. Subcommittee on Housing of the Committee on Banking and Currency of the US House of Representatives (6, 1955, 84th Congress, 1955), 45.

8. *Ibid.*, 55.

9. House Committee on Banking and Currency, Hearings and Reports of the Subcommitee on Housing (84th Congress, 1955), 22.

Chapter 6

The Urban Renewal Experience

The Housing Act of 1949 included the decision to begin Urban Renewal in Washington, which had been recommended by the DC Commissioners, a three-person board appointed by the president, and approved by the National Capital Planning Commission (NCPC). The responsibility for the Urban Renewal program in Washington, DC, was assigned to the DC Redevelopment Land Agency, which also was established by the Housing Act of 1949.

The first Urban Renewal site in Washington was in Southwest. Local officials and the NCPC agreed that the conditions in Southwest warranted first consideration for Urban Renewal because a high percentage of its dwellings faced the interiors of alleys and lacked central heat, indoor toilets, and electricity. Southwest had the highest crime rate in the city and the most overcrowding. There were many children living in the alleys who had serious health problems. In addition, Southwest Washington was close to the US Capitol building. Many people considered the conditions in Southwest to be a national disgrace that demanded prompt and drastic improvement. Urban Renewal was intended to eliminate the blight, provide improved housing conditions, and stabilize the city's economy.

The original Urban Renewal plan called for the rehabilitation of existing housing and the elimination of alley dwellings. In accordance with approved procedures, however, the DC Redevelopment Land Agency issued a public invitation to developers to submit proposals for the renewal of this land. A developer from Norfolk, Virginia submitted a proposal for the area between 4th Street and South Capitol Street, the railroad tracks, and G Street, known as Area B. The proposal included brand new apartments interspersed with town houses. The developer was willing to pay a higher price for the land than Urban Renewal officials had even considered on the condition that he could build all new housing rather than rehabilitate existing dwellings. The Urban Renewal officials, in consultation with city leaders, decided that it was a good idea to accept his proposal primarily because it would bring a high monetary return and thus assure the funding of other renewal areas. The acceptance of that proposal authorized the creation of high-rise buildings interspersed with town houses. Though it was clear that many existing residents would not be able to afford the new housing, the plan clearly met the Urban Renewal objective of a decent living environment. Some of the displaced families returned to the new public housing built adjacent to the Urban Renewal sites, but most of them moved to other parts of the city. Washington was segregated, but Urban Renewal officials expected Southwest to be a balanced community, with blacks and whites in the same apartment buildings.

Urban Renewal officials divided the Southwest area into three distinct Urban Renewal project areas for the purpose of slum clearance. The three areas included a total of twenty-five thousand residents and fourteen hundred businesses, all of which were scheduled for relocation. Each section was a distinct neighborhood, which made separate development feasible. Washington, DC, had the largest Urban Renewal Program in the country at the time.

The Relocation of Residents

Soon after the DC Redevelopment Land Agency selected its first executive director in 1950, I was invited to join the staff as director of relocation. It was my responsibility to select a staff to move families to affordable and decent housing and to help businesses find alternative locations. Though the regulations developed by the National Urban Renewal Administration clearly required that displaced families be moved to decent, safe, and sanitary housing that they could afford, the regulations did not suggest or require a process for achieving that objective.

People who lived in alleys spent many hours outside. There were generally only two rooms per apartment in the alleys, so many people, when the weather was good, were outside because it was too hot and close inside. People were outside even up until November.

The alleys were very small, about wide enough for one car. They had a kind of odor, a combination of outside toilets and garbage. Many of the toilets were stopped up. They ran into the sewer, but because there were multiple families using one toilet, it was a mess. Few residents made sure that the commodes were clean or flushed.

There was extensive alcohol use and people got sick as a result of over consumption. I was really shocked by the atmosphere. There was no greenery in the alleys, which was strange because Washington is a very green city. Nobody had a garden or flowers in the windows. There was a tension amongst residents, and few opportunities to do anything, two factors that helped to establish a depressing atmosphere.

My initial thought about the alleys was really a question: How can these people live like this? It was so dirty and drab. It had an air of rejection to it. There weren't many people smiling at each other. The alleys were unhappy places. Most families had little choice but to live there because the alleys were the only places that they could afford.

From the beginning it was clear that the success of the relocation process depended upon the ability of my staff to be patient and supportive of residents who faced this dramatic change. I spent many hours identifying the qualifications that were used in selecting personnel to interview families and to convince them that their lives could be improved by the changes in residence. We expected that some families would face serious difficulties and need special consideration. So I tried to find people who fit that model of warmth, understanding, and patience.

I found a woman who had worked during World War II in war housing, Mrs. Ella Foster. Mrs. Carrie Young had experience working with children and families in Southwest. Perry Holmes had experience working with families in school settings as a counselor. Miss Barbara Kemp had experience working in housing at the national level and I thought that would be helpful. Thomas O'Toole had worked for the IRS. Without exception these employees lived up to my highest expectations.

We had a number of training sessions to help us prepare for the relocation process. We addressed the issues of interviewing families, recording information, and asking personal questions without being too intrusive. We knew that it was important to make people feel comfortable. We had a teapot in the office and when families would come in to see the staff, we would give them a cup of tea.

The first thing we had to do was talk to the community about the plans for Urban Renewal. We went to churches and other institutions and discussed the relocation plan. We also visited each family. We knew which blocks were going to be worked on first, so scheduled visits accordingly. We prepared a form with names, addresses, places of employment, the number of people in the family, and all of the history that we could gain. We determined the services that were needed by the families, the part of the city to which they preferred to move, and when it might be convenient for them to move.

After conducting interviews family by family, we brought the information back to the office. We had one woman whose job was to look for a proper place for each family using the information we had been given. When she got the addresses and the telephone numbers of the agents, she would tell the appropriate relocation aide. The workers would then call the agent and tell them that they wanted to show a house.

People were frightened about moving. They were uncertain. That's one of the reasons that we took each family to look at the place where they would be moving. We not only took them to the house, but we also drove them around the neighborhood. Sometimes we took them two or three times to the same place just so they could become familiar with the surroundings.

We spent more time with alley dwellers than with people whose homes faced the streets. There were a number of families who visited apartments with us who were just awed by electric refrigerators. Most of them had ice boxes. These were people who had very little previous contact with comforts that today are considered standard. They needed extra help to adjust to the new environment and to operate some of the new equipment. Many of the people who lived facing the street did not need help to find a house. They were independent and they moved at their own initiative.

Procedures developed with our experiences. For example, we helped families to move from one room to a three-bedroom house. They couldn't use a three-bedroom house if they didn't have any furniture. So we appealed to the public for donations of home furnishings. The response was overwhelming. We were forced to obtain use of a warehouse to accommodate all of the gifts from generous people throughout the metropolitan area.

We sometimes had to take other unusual steps to help families meet the standard requirement for admission. In one instance, a family composed of a grandmother, mother, and son lived in a freestanding frame house that contained only one space heater. The windows and doors in the house were ill fitting and the crawl space was not enclosed, so that during the winter it was impossible to keep the house warm. The grandmother adopted her family's custom of sewing each family member into warm clothing when it was clear that winter had come and removing this clothing only when it was clear that spring had arrived. *The clothes had panels that were removed for cleaning and bathroom needs.*

By reason of income and family composition, this family met standard requirements for admission to public housing. We decided, however, that the family's experience might hinder their tenancy in public housing. With the cooperation of the Salvation Army, we furnished an apartment for them and provided this family a temporary dwelling in Southwest to help them adjust to conditions that were more commodious than those in their original home. Sure enough, six months later, the family had made a successful adjustment and was moved to a public housing dwelling. The family's tenancy, from all reports, was quite satisfactory.A blind man who lived alone occupied one alley dwelling. When asked about his preferences for a new place to live, he was uncertain. When asked where his physician was located he said, "I do not have a physician." He added, "When I began to become blind, I knew it was the work of the Lord. Seeing a doctor was not going to help."

We strongly suggested that he visit a public clinic in the Southwest area to get an opinion from the doctor in charge. He agreed. Sure enough, the visit resulted in an eye examination and the diagnosis was that he had cataracts. Shortly thereafter, the cataracts were removed, and the resident regained his sight and ultimately got a job. We located a suitable housing unit and the resident who "used to be blind" was successfully relocated.

Sometimes we found that families needed some public assistance. We even helped people find jobs. One woman who was on welfare and had four children asked for help in finding employment. I told her that a hospital (later called DC General) had advertised for nurses' aides. She went down there and she got the job. Her family subsequently showed the same ambition and drive and eventually completed college and attained professional employment. All four of her daughters became government employees.

Oftentimes I went with the relocation aides to interview families. One of the first times that I went into an alley I saw two ladies who were neighbors. One said to the other, "You know, I don't have any bread and I don't have a penny to buy a loaf of bread." Bread cost a quarter in those days. The downstairs lady said, "I don't have much money left but here's a quarter." It was a good first impression. I thought that the folks in alleys had good relationships. But the more I went into alleys, the more I heard reports that somebody had been arrested the night before for beating his wife, or that somebody had been caught stealing in one of the stores in the area.

Nearly one-third of the families that we moved out of Southwest were relocated into public housing. The National Capital Housing Authority stood ready to honor the priority of displaced families, but required that they meet all standard of the requirements for admission. For example, one of the requirements for admission was that a man and woman who were living together must be legally married. Some of the couples facing displacement who were otherwise eligible for public housing were encouraged to marry, and in some cases, were driven to nearby Rockville, Maryland, where they could be married within an hour. No unmarried couples were referred for public housing.

Most of the other families moved to privately owned dwellings where rents were modest. A smaller number of families were too large to be housed properly in public housing or average privately owned dwellings. We had one family of fourteen that we were required to move to decent, safe, and sanitary housing, which they could afford, but we didn't have any houses that were suitable for that large of a group. So, we went to the Housing and Home Finance Agency (HHFA) because they had a demonstration fund for just such problems. We told them our predicament and asked them whether we could rent privately owned houses with five or six bedrooms that would be large enough to accommodate this family. That request set the stage for the addition of a new program called "scattered site" public housing, in which the housing authorities would buy or rent houses from private owners for larger families.

The Relocation of Businesses

There were fourteen hundred businesses that ranged from very small operations to large warehouses that we helped to find new locations. Most did not remain in Southwest. Several food wholesalers bought a piece of land in Southwest right next to the railroad tracks where they erected a building. But they were among the few to remain. Southwest had quite a number of restaurants and most of the restaurants were either relocated down on the waterfront or to the lower part of Southwest down near Fort McNair.

Some business owners were very much opposed to Urban Renewal. But when we told them that we would pay all of the moving costs, they softened a bit. Overall there was no concerted opposition. We tried to move businesses to commercial spots where there was a buying public.

They had their choice of where to go. We took them around to look at places to help them determine the best place to move.

In keeping with the Urban Renewal Plan, a big shopping center was built in Southwest at 4th and M Streets to accommodate some businesses. Most of the businesses that had been located in Southwest before Urban Renewal couldn't afford to move in there. They weren't the kind of establishments that would survive in that shopping center because the rent was too high.

Many of the smaller stores were replaced by chain stores such as People's Drug Store (later called CVS), and Safeway. There were fewer, smaller stores in Southwest after Urban Renewal. But that was true in most parts of the city.

As on-site representatives of the DC Redevelopment Land Agency, we also assumed the responsibility of seeing to the proper demolition of vacated buildings. That work was supervised by the deputy director of our unit, William Neal Goodson, whose job was to make certain that no family was inconvenienced by the demolition and that the community environment was protected from vandals and despoilers. As with the relocation of families and businesses, the demolition was accomplished with minimal friction and no major calamities.

I was most fortunate to have a staff that was able and willing to help displaced families cope with this significant change in their lives. We felt that we were helping people to prepare for a new environment. I liked the idea of eliminating slums. It was helpful to get people who were in substandard housing moved to housing that was standard. My feeling was that the move would improve the social conditions and the lives of individual families as well.

Dilemma of Urban Renewal

Some organizations, including civil rights advocates, housing advocates, the local Urban League, and the National Association for the Advancement of Colored People (NAACP) said that Urban Renewal was "Negro removal" because a substantial number of the people who were affected by it were black. They thought it would be impossible to be fair and helpful to people with that big a project.

In a sense, Urban Renewal began the troubles of public housing. After that point, most people displaced by public development were given priority admission to public housing. On the other hand, it might be said that before Urban Renewal, when the government chose to begin a public works project, there was no requirement for relocation. People living in housing where public facilities were planned were simply told to get out. For instance, when the government built the Supreme Court, the people who lived there were simply kicked out. There was no organized relocation for them. The government took the land under the power of eminent domain.

In many cities, public housing was the main source of housing for families that had been displaced by Urban Renewal. There were many private rental housing owners who were reluctant to accept families who had been displaced from slum areas where "crime and immorality" were reportedly rampant. To increase the housing available from privately owned rental housing, it was often necessary to urge cooperation of the real estate industry. The effectiveness of the efforts to increase opportunities to move the displaced to privately owned housing was mixed. In some cities where displaced families were rehoused in privately owned rental housing, there were protests from existing residents. In Washington, DC, there were several complaints. On a few occasions I invited the protesting residents to visit the new neighbors. Though some protesters refused, most accepted their new neighbors. In most instances, the dissenters found their new neighbors to be civil and aspiring to achieve a state of stable and independent living.

The major complaints we received about Urban Renewal, however, were from advocates who represented the displaced. Most advocates wanted to raise the level of funds given to residents for moving. Whereas the Urban Renewal Administration was not authorized to provide social services, local renewal agencies were encouraged to hire personnel who were acquainted with the social service network and who could establish relations that would be beneficial to displaced families. After all, many residents of slum areas that were scheduled for Urban Renewal had been clients of social service agencies for many years.

As with any major national program, there were some variations in the interpretation of regulations. To eliminate misunderstanding, the regional offices of the HHFA scheduled regular meetings with local officials. These opportunities to share experiences as well as to discuss regulations proved to be effective in improving services.

Chapter 7

Programs of the Great Society

With an estimated two million residents, public housing provided a significant source of housing for people with low incomes,[1] but the program experienced a change during the late 1950s and early 1960s. The altered regulations that resulted from the Housing Act of 1949 changed the resident profile of public housing.

By the early 1960s, more than half of all families in public housing were nonwhite, primarily because minorities, particularly African Americans, lived in areas that were affected by Urban Renewal.[2] African Americans were still three times as likely to live in poverty as whites.

The percentage of single-parent families had not risen too much in public housing population (around one-quarter). The number of public housing residents who received welfare benefits had also increased to nearly fifty percent.[3]

The 1960s

Equal rights for blacks and whites became an important issue for American society. The 1954 Supreme Court decision *in Brown v. Board of Education* officially turned the tide, but it had limited immediate impact. It was the civil rights movement of the 1960s that brought dramatic changes in both public policy and social relationships. No longer limited to segregation and official social restrictions, the movement challenged the culture, which sanctioned extensive mistreatment in even the most rudimentary transactions.

The images of struggle in the streets, in restaurants, and on buses became an important symbol in the fight against oppression. The quest for equality was not, however, limited to public places. Inequality pushed deeper into the fabric of American life than simple segregation. Economic, health, and educational disparity between white and African Americans was great. As the Kerner Commission termed it, two worlds existed, black and white, which were separate and unequal.

The staggering disparity between blacks and whites aroused great concern in the public sector. Many officials felt that government action was necessary to create an "even playing field."

Unfortunately, changes in the law and new interpretations of the Constitution did not change the realities of American life. With the Presidency of John F. Kennedy, government response to the plight of economically disadvantaged minorities increased. When the Kennedy administration was cut short because of the President's assassination, Lyndon Johnson assumed the office with the clear intention of making a stronger government push to eradicate areas of denied opportunity and encourage the poor and minorities to seek a path to higher achievement.

The United States had emerged as a dominant force in world affairs, yet domestic conflict plagued the country. The progression toward a "Great Society" became a main theme of the Johnson administration.

The Economic Opportunity Act of 1964

The first major effort by the Johnson administration to create equality was the Economic Opportunity Act of 1964 (EOA). Unlike the previous major urban initiative, Urban Renewal, the EOA focused primarily on social improvement by using the encouragement of community action. *Maximum feasible participation* was the legislative catch phrase that defined the essence of the Act.

The EOA authorized the establishment of Office of Economic Opportunity (OEO), a federal organization, to oversee the creation and implementation of various initiatives. Municipal governments and local community groups were encouraged to design their own programs

The reach of the programs created and run by OEO was truly great. The program sponsored a Youth Job Corps and Work Training Program that brought practical skills to young people between the ages of sixteen and twenty-one. Study programs for children with low incomes who desired a college education were implemented at schools with large populations of poor children. Adults were provided with opportunities to further their education. Community leaders were encouraged to organize against local initiatives that did not seem to meet the needs or were diametrically opposed to the needs of their communities.

The OEO also created two programs that still exist. The Volunteers in Service to America (VISTA) was the predecessor to AmeriCorps, which encourages young people to become active, particularly in urban communities. Head Start was created to give underprivileged preschoolers and toddlers access to educational and nutritional opportunities.

Much of the support for the Poverty Program (as the EOA was also known) came from local leaders involved in the Ford Foundation–supported "Gray Area Program." This program, which had been underway for several years in Boston, Massachusetts; New Haven, Connecticut; Philadelphia, Pennsylvania; Oakland, California; and Washington, DC, and produced much of the blueprint for the National War on Poverty. Three of the major objectives of the Gray Area Program were to activate the poor to organize and advocate better opportunities for themselves, to seek a greater understanding of their needs by way of dedicated legal representation, and to increase emphasis on the need for improved training and nurturing of children at every stage of development.

The Housing and Urban Development Act of 1965

The year after the creation of the EOA, President Johnson won support for an important bill for sustained, long-term government action in urban affairs. The Department of Housing and Urban Development (HUD) formed under the Housing and Urban Development Act of 1965. Whereas previous administrations had encouraged legislative action on urban issues, the Johnson administration sought to show a lasting commitment to urban and housing issues by creating an executive department.[4]

A department to plan and coordinate the nation's important urban initiatives had long been proposed. It was clear that previous urban solutions and strategies had not been completely effective. Ultimately, the movement became strong enough to convince Congress to approve the establishment of the US Department of Housing and Urban Development.

HUD was intended to "allow Federal participation in metropolitan area thinking and planning" through work with education, health, employment, and social services.[5] The plan for the Department included all organizations that were associated with housing, including the Federal Housing Administration (FHA) and the Public Housing Administration (PHA).[6]

Robert C. Weaver became the first secretary and the first African American to head a cabinet-level department. Weaver envisioned a department with a uniformly accepted set of policies to be implemented by an able and intelligent staff. He was convinced that housing and other social programs required coordination at every level government.[7]

In addition to the creation of HUD, the Housing and Urban Development Act of 1965 provided for the creation of new public housing. Over a four-year period, the Act called for the construction of 240,000 brand new units. It also provided for 15,000 units to be bought from existing housing and 10,000 units to be leased from already existing housing.[8]

Model Cities

A year after the creation HUD, President Johnson called for the creation of a new program to battle the still ailing ghettoes of America. Both Urban Renewal and the EOA had provided a basis by which to move forward in the development of new techniques to solve urban problems, yet much remained to be done.

The Model Cities Program, which was created by the Demonstration Cities and Metropolitan Development Act of 1966, synthesized the EOA and Urban Renewal to provide a more comprehensive and coordinated approach. Both physical and social problems were addressed in legislative language with a less fragmented organizational base.

Supporters of the Demonstration Cities Program, as it was sometimes called, included the US Conference of Mayors, AFL-CIO, National Legislative Committee of the American Institute of Planners, the Americans for Democratic Action, and the National Housing Conference. The architects and coordinators of the plan were certain that with the combined physical and social focus, the new program would provide a stronger basis for improved change in both the physical and social conditions of our cities.

Tenant Unrest in Public Housing

As the 1960s progressed, the rent paid by residents of public housing throughout the country ceased to cover the operating costs of projects. The reduced level of Congressional appropriation combined with the level of inflation increased rent significantly for some residents. Rising rents, however, were not accompanied by a rise in income for public housing residents.[10]

The government, however, was no ordinary landlord. Dissatisfied with their predicament, the tenants of public housing all across the country protested.

Organizations such as the National Tenants Organization sponsored rent strikes in cities such as Chicago and St. Louis to demand the reduction of rent for people who were unable to afford the rising rents. The Housing Act of 1949 had begun the slow decline in the number of working, two-parent families in public housing. The new population was more susceptible to economic frustration and ready to join the protest.

The Brooke Amendments

Edward Brooke, a Republican from Massachusetts and the first African American Senator since Reconstruction, was concerned about the predicament of public housing tenants. Although fiscally conservative, Brooke felt a great need to promote social equality.

In 1969, Brooke sponsored the first of three amendments that would drastically change the public housing system. This amendment ensured that all public housing residents who were not on public assistance would pay no more than twenty-five percent of their incomes for rent. Then, in 1970, Senator Brooke introduced an amendment that increased the number of exemptions from the income of tenants. These amendments caused the implementation of an operating subsidy that was to be provided by the Federal government. The result was a reduction in the base of income that would be considered by authorities for payment of rent. Finally, in 1971, Brooke introduced an amendment that allowed recipients of public assistance to receive the same assurance of low rent guaranteed under the 1969 amendment. The impact of this amendment was to reduce the rents of recipients of public assistance to the minimum level, thus reducing the funds received from rents that were available for the operation and management of public housing. With decreased rental income and insufficient government subsidies, many housing authorities were unable to maintain properties in satisfactory condition. As conditions deteriorated many families moved, even if it meant paying a much higher percentage of their income for rent.

Notes

1. Willman, John B., *The Department of Housing and Urban Development.* (New York: Frederick A. Praeger, 1967), 19.
2. Statistics Branch, *Families Living in Low Rent Public Housing.* (Washington, DC: HUD, 1960–1964).
3. *Ibid.*
4. Willman, John B., *The Department of Housing and Urban Development* (New York: Frederick A. Praeger, 1967), 22.
5. Willman, *The Department of Housing and Urban Development*, 38.
6. *Ibid.* 38.
7. *Ibid.*, 45.
8. *Ibid.*
9. US Department of Housing and Urban Development, *Programs of HUD* (Washington, DC: Department of Housing and Urban Development, 1967), 21.
10. House Subcommittee on Housing of the Committee on Banking and Currency, 194.

Chapter 8

The Poverty Program

I served as Assistant Commissioner for Relocation at the Urban Renewal Administration and had held that position for a little less than three years when I was asked to take a leave of absence to prepare a plan for the Ford Foundation's Gray Area Program. The Gray Area Program was initiated by the vice president of the Ford Foundation, Paul Ylvisaker, who thought it was imperative that poor people in American cities have a responsible role in their own employment and education. The program was conducted in five cities: Boston; Philadelphia; New Haven, Connecticut; Washington, DC; and Oakland, California.

The major objectives of the Gray Area Program were to organize the poor to advocate better opportunities for themselves, to seek more understanding of their needs through dedicated legal representation and to give increased emphasis to the need for improved training and nurturing of children at every stage of development.

The program sought to improve the quality of services offered to impoverished people by including them in the planning of services so that they could develop knowledge to bring themselves out of impoverishment.

UPO

When the poverty program was passed by Congress, the United Planning Organization (UPO) became the poverty agency for the Washington metropolitan area. UPO's original purpose was, as its name suggests, to be a planning organization for the city, to develop data on both need and resources, and to put the resources where the need was greatest. However, when we were designated the poverty agency for the metropolitan area, it became a service organization. We received millions of dollars to develop and aid a myriad of programs.

As executive director of the UPO working to prepare an application for the Ford Foundation Gray Area Program funds, I had an opportunity to study the social and physical conditions that beset Washington, DC, and its surrounding communities in Maryland and Virginia.

Poverty and its attendant problems continued to be most severe in the inner city, concentrated in the central section of Northwest Washington and areas of Southeast Washington that were not separated from the city by the Anacostia River. The Far Southeast and Northeast areas both had developed slowly prior to World War II. Most of the housing that had been built before the war was single-family dwellings. The new public and privately owned subsidized housing brought major influx of poor families to the area.

The UPO served the metropolitan area. We worked in the Shaw Area of Washington, DC, the 14th Street Area, Southwest Washington, and Southeast Washington west of the Anacostia River. We had one agency in Anacostia called the Southeast Neighborhood House. We also had programs in Montgomery County and Prince George's County, Maryland, and Arlington and Alexandria, Virginia. We encouraged the formation of community action centers, which served as coordinators of the program. Those neighborhood centers were the operative arms of the poverty program.

At first, we notified community organizations that already existed about our desire to help fund them. We gave them information about what we wanted to do and asked whether they were interested in participating. If they were interested, they submitted proposals to us, and if we accepted them, we funded them.

We started several programs, some of which are still around. For example, the Head Start Program in Washington, DC, started in our office. We created and were also responsible for the administration of Neighborhood Youth Corps, which provided employment opportunities for impoverished youth and in the process tried to get them to help their families and community.

The Neighborhood Legal Service was a required component of the program. Its purpose was to provide legal services for poor people who had no funds but who had been, in many documented instances, treated either illegally or unfairly by agencies that were responsible for providing them with services. The Neighborhood Legal Services also helped people who had been arrested or convicted of crimes. In addition, we started credit unions in many sections of the city to help residents save money and make loans to each other. Most important, the credit unions were run by people living in the community. Their boards of directors and many of the staff were recruited from the neighborhoods.

We wanted to help poor residents become engaged in the process of government and with the private agencies that served them. To a certain extent, this came to pass. Residents became more active in tenant associations. Some joined neighborhood civic associations, what at that time long had been established as the principal civic power in the city. A few residents became members of the boards of directors of city-wide groups that were urging more opportunities for the poor. The increased participation generated a more hopeful spirit as many people for the first time sat down for serious conversations with government and private agency leaders. Some of the people who went through that process became leaders, including one woman who became a member of the first elected school board.

However, the poverty program did not address what I would now consider the major problem: that is, the strengthening of families and communities not only to influence public policy programs but also to influence the quality of the lives within the families and within the communities.

The Perspective of an Executive Director

In 1969, I accepted appointment by DC Mayor Walter E. Washington to the newly authorized position of Assistant to the Mayor for Housing Programs. This assignment included responsibility for administration of the City Planning Office, and Historic Preservation Office, and the city's Model Cities Program.

In addition, I was assigned to serve as the Mayor's alternate to the NCPC. My responsibilities were increased in 1970 with my assignment by the mayor to serve as the executive director of the National Capital Housing Authority.

The urban disorder that followed the assassination of Martin Luther King, Jr., left its imprint on Washington, DC. Some business spaces were so badly burned or vandalized that the restoration cost estimates were far beyond the assets of the owner. Lending institutions, equally uncertain, were not eager to provide funds for repair and new equipment. Some residents and businesses that were frightened by the violence and extensive damage moved to the suburbs.

Public housing also felt the quake of unrest. It was hard hit by the increase of one-parent, welfare-dependent families. As the resident population slowly came to include more and more of the poorest families, it lost many of its moderate-income families. Public housing managers reported that single mothers, under constant requirement to see that there was enough to eat and to make sure that children were properly cared for, had little energy to do the maintenance required of tenants for their dwellings. Maintenance requests from tenants and complaints increased just as rental income to cover maintenance and management costs diminished. This new stressful work environment encouraged many long-time housing employees to retire. Some of the younger workers found other employment. As repairs on public housing dwellings were delayed because of staff shortages, vacancies increased. Public housing in Washington, DC, had never experienced such persistent and large-scale problems.

When I became the director of public housing, the worst public housing in the city was in Southeast and Southwest. Returning the dwellings to livable conditions required extra effort from maintenance personnel, an extra dose of patience from residents, and increased funding to make up for lost time. With outstanding assistance from Deputy Director Monteria Ivey, and Director of Management George Miner, we conducted special meetings with management, maintenance staff, and residents on every housing development. We urged both staff and residents to suggest means of coping with the problem. Conditions varied from property to property and suggested solutions also differed somewhat.

Some of the Washington, DC, public housing tenants, with encouragement from the National Tenants Organization, called a rent strike. Their position was simply that until the National Capital Housing Authority made dwellings livable they would pay no rent. Tenant rent was not adequate to pay for the high cost of maintenance. The conditions of the dwellings were so poor because we didn't have the money to deal with all of the problems. With the increase in the number of single parents, the labor from the family to maintain the property likewise diminished. And there were subsequent increases in calls for maintenance from increasingly female-headed households. They had a lot of responsibility and heavy burdens to bear, and maintenance was not their highest priority.

My responsibility as the new public housing director was to find ways to minimize the problems, bring an end to the strike, and reorganize the program to avoid future breakdowns in management. I took several steps to bring an end to the strike, return the dwellings to livable condition, collect unpaid rents from strikers, and return Housing Authority-resident relations to their former mutually supportive standing.

One evening, the striking tenants invited me to a meeting at a Catholic church on East Capitol Street on Capitol Hill. I was to speak before the president of the National Tenants Organization, which had started in Harlem and assisted tenants across the country. After I gave my speech, the head of the National Tenants Organization and said, "You are poor people. You shouldn't have to pay any rent at all." And of course I had already said my piece, so I couldn't make any response. As I was getting ready to leave, the people in the audience jammed the door so that I couldn't get out. They wanted me to promise that they wouldn't have to pay all their back rent and whatever. I told them that I would talk to each one of the tenants and we could arrange for them to pay it as it was convenient according to their income, which I did.

There was no disagreement, however, with the idea that resident participation was an absolute necessity if improvements were to be achieved. New regulations were issued to reinstate regular staff inspections of dwellings so as to note both maintenance requirements and the level of resident care of their dwellings. We then met with tenants to arrange for needed repairs and agreements for improved resident care. To engage residents in the process of improvement, we began a series of neighborhood maintenance events. On Saturdays, residents and maintenance staff came together to paint the exteriors and interiors of dwellings. Often participants would also prepare sandwiches and cold drinks for everyone who was working to improve the housing. Pat Nixon, the First Lady, visited the Barry Farm Public Housing Development once as residents and staff joined to improve the project.

The response to this new approach to maintenance was enthusiastic. The relationships that developed between staff and residents began to improve other aspects of the public housing program, including rent payment. As we worked to improve conditions, we held interviews with residents whose rents were unpaid to reach agreements for the payment of current rents. Though the process took several months, most strikers accepted the agreements and most of them were true to their word. Within twelve months, the problems began to recede.

By the early 1970s, drug sales and use had become a major problem in public housing. In the Lincoln Heights Development where I had selected the 440 families when it was initially occupied in 1944, there was trouble. One of its three-story apartment buildings was in such a state of disrepair that most of the legal residents had moved. Soon the building was in the possession of drug dealers and users. Apparently neither the police, agency staff, nor tenants wanted to confront the dangerous new inhabitants whose reputation was so well known.

A call from a local business leader who manufactured prefabricated housing raised the idea of training prisoners in Washington's facility at Lorton, Virginia to make housing parts and receive compensation. I thought it was a great idea and raised it with the director of the Department of Corrections, who though the idea was good but that the dangers both to prisoners and staff not worth it.

Because I knew that our prisoners included some young people with training and experience in housing construction, I asked the Chief of Corrections if he thought he could organize a team of inmates to remodel an apartment building. He agreed to try. A few weeks later we signed an agreement, including wages set aside for inmates on their release, for the team to repair the building at Lincoln Heights. When the Lorton team arrived, the intruders left. When the Lorton team completed the job, legal tenants moved in and a community eyesore had been removed.

I had two experiences while I was director that helped me realize just where public housing was going and why it was going in that direction. There was a woman in one of the developments in Southwest who was a recovered mental patient who had a child. Mother and child lived in an apartment on the third or fourth floor of one of our public housing developments.

The child, who was no more than age ten, had part of a train track with sharp points. Every day he would go down the hallway and drag the track along the wall. Eventually there was a deep groove. The neighbors began to complain. We talked to his mother about the situation and she became defensive. Ultimately we sought her eviction after further complaints from other tenants. The case went to court and the judge ruled that we couldn't evict her because the woman had no other place to go. That was when I realized that public housing had become the last resort.

I subsequently had lunch with the judge, and he told me that he thought that public housing was intended to do just what he ordered, that is, to take care of the people whom nobody else would take. We had come to a point at which a judge had the authority to require us to accept families whom we didn't want or who would not have been accepted otherwise. Generally, if people acted in ways that were destructive, we asked them to leave. We were still sending people out to inspect people's houses then, but it didn't seem to matter.

Around Christmas one year, I received a call late at night. There was a fire in an eight-story public housing building in Southwest on M Street. It happened that a family had bought two new mattresses for Christmas and put their old mattresses in the hall. The discarded mattresses ended up in the elevator. We never did find out who put them there, nor did we find out who set them on fire. That fire caused the metal in all four elevators to warp, leaving about 150 families who lived in that complex without elevators from Christmas until March. Though this experience was most unusual, I cite it to indicate that a few residents had begun to make life more difficult for their neighbors.

A Study of Anacostia

The office of the mayor asked the planning office, of which I was head, to conduct a study of the Far Southeast section of the city, where increasing concern about crime and other social issues had been made public. The resulting report to Mayor Washington, titled Far Southeast 1970, *revealed some startling facts.*

The population of the area had increased from 79,170 in 1950 to 116,200 in 1970. The median age for the Far Southeast area was twenty, whereas the median age in the rest of the city was thirty. Slightly more than fifteen percent of the Far Southeast population was under five years of age.[1]

The city's zoning commission, in response to the urgent need for increasing housing, had designated seventy-five percent of the area for the construction of mostly garden-type apartment dwellings and city-wide zoning reserved eighty percent of the land for single-family houses and only twenty percent for apartments.[2]

Rental housing came to be more highly subsidized in Far Southeast than in other sections of the city. The report recommended a change in the city's zoning so as to permit the development of more single-family housing. This effort to turn the tide of largely subsidized rental housing, was officially approved, but the response from potential developers was hesitant. The area was, by then, on its way to becoming not only home to more of the city's poor but also the area most readily identified by the media and citizens as the most crime ridden and unhealthy. Just the name "Far Southeast" was used to describe the worst urban conditions imaginable.

Notes

1. Office of Assistant to the Mayor for Housing Programs, Community Renewal Program, *F-SE, Washington's Far Southeast in 1971: A Report to the Honorable Mayor Walter E. Washington.* Washington, DC: Government Printing Office, 1970).
2. *Ibid.*

Chapter 9

The Decline of Public Housing

By 1973, more than half of all impoverished people were living in metropolitan areas. By 1974, the rate of poverty for children was actually higher than that for the elderly.[1]

Many of the programs that had been created during the Johnson administration were regarded with disfavor by the Nixon administration, which determined that significant changes in the system of urban aid were necessary. The Housing and Community Development Act of 1974 enacted such a change. The Act created the Community Development Block Grant, which consolidated the funding of the Model Cities Program and Urban Renewal, as well as other less well known programs into one federal block grant.

In addition, and perhaps more important, the Housing and Community Development Act created a new program for housing low-income people. It amended the Housing Act of 1937 to create a voucher system that was intended to help qualified applicants move into privately owned, federally approved housing. Instead of replacing public housing, Section 8 was an alternative for housing the poor.

Never during the planning of public housing could the architects have imagined the devastation of the 1970s and 1980s. It seemed almost out of a horror film: the death, the drugs, and the sheer poverty that blanketed so many cities. The situation was so overwhelming, it seemed that there was nothing to be done. Poverty had come to dominate much of urban life in a manner not seen since the Depression. In spite of all of the preceding Great Society Programs and an abundance of privately funded efforts to serve the urban poor, the problems were more resistant to remedy than ever before.

By the 1970s, urban public housing seemed to be in a state of siege as deterioration and vacancies increased and rent payments were more difficult to obtain. Public housing became synonymous with despair. As families with severe problems began to predominate the system, families with the means to leave did so. In earlier days, public housing had blended into its surroundings. By the 1970s, it was easily identifiable. Garden style walk-ups and towering high rises came to characterize much of the urban public housing system. Much of it was vacant and deteriorated. Walls were covered with graffiti. Even the children at play seemed to be reluctant, always ready to take flight if violence erupted.

Parklands

The history of the Parklands Development in Southeast Washington, DC and the changes it experienced over a period of more than fifty years provide a good example of the broad impact of clustering thousands of the poorest of the poor. Parklands, a privately owned, garden-type rental development of nearly two thousand dwellings was built in the 1940s for moderate- to middle-income black families. It was built on a hilly site that previously had been vacant. The development was built under the FHA 608 program, which encouraged new construction by insuring one hundred percent of the mortgage, thus encouraging developers to build without investing their own capital.

The newly built Parklands attracted an enthusiastic group of younger black couples. The modern, well-built dwellings, most of which possessed fine views of the surrounding hilly terrain, was a welcome change to many. Some of the new residents came from older sections of the city where housing had begun to decay and social problems had increased. For many, Parklands was the next best thing to moving to the suburbs. At that time, there were few opportunities for black families to move to the suburbs. Parklands was only a short distance from the Washington, DC-Prince Georges County, Maryland line.

About the same time that Parklands was built, the National Capital Housing Authority began construction of a two hundred and fifty unit development called Frederick Douglass Dwellings. It was built on vacant land just a block from Parklands. This development, built for World War II workers, also attracted young families whose chief income was from employment in one of the certified war preparation activities. For at least two decades, these two developments enjoyed a stable coexistence. Both were in demand. Neither had vacancies, vandalism, or significant problems. Both were well maintained and offered an attractive physical appearance.

In 1957, the Housing Authority began construction of another public housing development adjacent to both Parklands and Frederick Douglass Dwellings. This new development, called Stanton Dwellings, was built to accommodate families that had been displaced by public works, including the Southwest Urban Renewal Program. For nearly a decade these three developments were reasonably stable. The Frederick Douglass development was later converted from temporary war housing to permanent public housing.

As the requirements for admission began to favor those in greatest need, subtle changes began in the neighborhood. Crime slowly increased. The number of young men who hung out on the corners increased, and the Housing Authority began to experience problems collecting rent. The more stable residents at Parklands and Frederick Douglass began to move. Families that moved into Frederick Douglass Dwellings were increasingly single-parent families with many on welfare. Parklands, without rental subsidies, found its efforts to attract moderate- to middle-income families increasingly difficult.

By the 1980s, life in the Parklands area had changed measurably. Crime was rampant and businesses began to suffer. Ultimately the Parklands development had as many as fifteen hundred vacant apartments. This was only a portion of Ward 8 in Washington, DC, where there came to be approximately ten thousand vacant apartments. The ward lost nearly twenty thousand residents during the decade.

Public Housing Statistics

Where once high standards had been upheld, both in the admission of residents and for the maintenance of public housing, serious change had come. Housing authorities were forced to alter their mission from helping return poor people to mainstream life to serving as the housing of last resort for the poorest of the poor. Public housing was the bottom of the heap, the lowest level of housing for families that had no other options. The only requirement for admission, in many locales, was to meet income requirements, which, as a result of decreased standards, were proportionately lower than ever.

The statistics from the late 1970s that describe the public housing population are certainly evidence of the system's diminished status. By 1979, eighty-eight percent of the resident families in public housing earned less than ten thousand dollars a year, but ninety-seven percent of families that entered public housing earned under than amount. In 1979, the median income for nonelderly families in public housing was $5,560. For those entering public housing, the median income was $4,857. More than half of all of the nonelderly families continued to be single parents, particularly mothers, with children. In some areas, almost three-quarters (and sometimes more) of the residents were on some form of public assistance. More than half of the public housing population was minority.[2]

These changes can be explained only as a result of the changes in policy that controlled standards of admission to public housing.

Changing Cities

The growing intensity of impoverishment in many urban areas, particularly those with public and subsidized housing, was even more shocking because of the great prosperity that existed elsewhere. There was a clear and ever-widening gap emerging between the rich and the poor as the poor moved into the cities and the nonpoor moved out.

As heavy industry began to leave the major cities, the economy of the country became increasingly dependent upon a fast-growing service industry. Unskilled workers were unable to secure other employment. The result of such a shift was tremendous. Economic problems caused many marriages to falter and seemed to discourage new marriages. More children were born out of wedlock. More mothers sought welfare. That part of the poor urban population that had found marginal employment as day workers found themselves working less often. Their infrequent and small paychecks dwindled. The descent to dependency was inevitable.

Explanations of the phenomena varied. Some experts insisted on structural inequalities to explain the proliferation of so many poor, urban blacks. Others could see no structural reason that had precipitated widespread urban inequality. Extremists began to proffer genetic makeup as an explanation. Many people, however, simply felt that it was the responsibility of the poor to raise themselves out of the horrors that had resulted from their own high level of disorder. Eventually the poor came to be termed the *underclass*, a designation that emphasized their permanence.

After the Carter administration ended in 1981, the Reagan Presidency began with a commitment to a conservative agenda. The great push of the Reagan administration was to limit the reach of the Federal government, to allow increased state and private control for many human service programs. The government efforts to help the poor had expanded greatly since the 1960s because of many efforts, including the War on Poverty. The Reagan administration felt that true change could be effected only with local and state initiatives.

The belief in the American ideals of equality and strict Constitutional principles characterized much of the thinking of the Reagan administration. Everything was in place for a fair and equal society. There was no reason to believe that any particular group of people was uniformly discriminated against or lacked opportunities that would keep them from achieving the American Dream. The individual, and the individual alone, could exact the will to succeed in this environment. This brand of conservatism expressed in no uncertain terms the belief that individual human achievement is a product of disciplined courage and initiative. Most of those who earnestly believed such philosophy could not imagine living in a society in which the most fundamental opportunities to achieve and succeed are denied or at least discouraged.

Omnibus Act of 1981

The Omnibus Act of 1981 was the first major piece of legislation that was enacted by the Reagan administration to promote a shift in government function. With regard to federally sponsored housing, the Act abandoned any illusion that such housing could or should be used to integrate the poor into mainstream life. The unabashed determination to make public and Section 8 housing exclusively for the extremely impoverished came in a revision of language in the Housing Act of 1937.

In testimony concerning the Omnibus Act, Reagan administration officials devoted substantial energy to describing the many unnecessary amenities, particularly in Section 8 housing, such as swimming pools, and carpeting that residents were provided. These amenities, according to administration officials, prevented the use of funds on housing for even more impoverished people. Even worse, according to the same officials, too much of the federally subsidized housing was given to people who did not deserve it. There were too many people in severe need of housing to permit funds to be used for families whose need was not acute.

The Omnibus Act of 1981 prompted strong action. The legislation allowed the admission of many homeless individuals and families who might otherwise not have gained admission. At the same time, funds for federally subsidized housing, in particular Section 8, were reduced significantly. The Act halted all funds that had been designated for the construction of new housing under Section 8 provisions.

In addition to the major assault on federal involvement in public and subsidized housing, the Omnibus Act of 1981 combined several programs related to urban affairs into eight block grants. The Reagan administration felt that government programs had become too large and cumbersome and that they needed to be trimmed to allow state and local, private and government agencies to make more decisions and to take some responsibility for urban problems. Under the new law, states were required to develop comprehensive plans to ensure that proposed activities would be coordinated properly. Programs lost funds because of federal cuts in spending and were rarely supplemented by state governments to ensure continuous benefits.

The responses of the states were varied. Over all, there was a concerted effort to increase the number of Section 8 units. Because new construction for Section 8 developments was eliminated, the use of this provision was confined to existing privately owned developments that accepted Section 8 certificates. In some cities the opportunities for the use of Section 8 certificates were centered in areas where public housing and existing Section 8 housing were concentrated. Many owners of private housing that was located adjacent to public housing were unable to attract market-rate renters. In desperation they accepted Section 8 certificates. The result was the gradual concentration of hundreds, even thousands of poor and troubled families in adjacent dwellings.

Segregation in Public Housing

One thing was certain with regard to housing the urban poor during the 1980s, and that was racial segregation. In 1985, *The Dallas Morning News* conducted a survey of forty-seven public housing projects throughout the country. Its findings, published in a series of reports, painted a picture of severe inequality in a system that was already beset with serious financial shortcomings.

The study found that predominantly white projects were in superior condition and location,"[3] were located closer to services, and had more amenities compared to projects that housed mostly blacks and Hispanics. Not a single observed project was fully integrated. Less than two decades prior to the analysis, the Fair Housing Act had been created to ensure that such segregation on the basis of race would not take place. However, there seemed to be few, if any, mechanisms to ensure the enforcement of such laws.

According to *The Dallas Morning News*, under the Reagan administration, the Justice Department had adopted very strict interpretations of federal civil rights laws. As a result of these new standards, violations of housing discrimination laws were extremely difficult to prove and even harder to remedy.

The article revealed the findings of an unpublished report that had been conducted by HUD in 1980. The report presented information on the effect of newly built subsidized housing on school segregation. The study, which examined the metropolitan areas of Denver, St. Louis, Phoenix, and Columbus, Ohio, found that "almost every single unit of subsidized housing that was built had the effect of increasing school segregation."[4]

Though public housing had an extensive waiting list that included mostly minorities, Section 8 housing tended to be found in areas with less concentrated poverty and a large number of white families, who constituted nearly eighty-five percent of the population. In other forms of assisted housing, such as certificate, voucher programs, and private, project-based programs, a significant majority of those served were white as well.[5]

The Dallas Morning News also criticized the extreme concentration of subsidized housing, particularly public housing, within urban areas. The city of Dallas, which claimed forty-nine percent of the total metropolitan area population, contained ninety-six percent of the total amount of subsidized housing. It seemed that cities were harboring an undue share of the burden of financially deprived public housing dwellers.[6]

A study conducted in 1994, which used census data from 1990, found serious segregation based on economic and racial attributes. According to the study, census

> . . . tracts that have less than a 1% African American residents have projects in which 71% of the tenants are white. Tracts that have 70% or more African American population have tenants who are 92% African American.[8]

Census tracts with higher percentages of blacks also tended to have larger public housing projects. These projects tended to be severely impoverished.

Tracts with low levels of poverty have higher proportions of white tenants, and tracts with high levels of poverty are almost exclusively African American . . . . The majority of African Americans living in public housing projects in the United States are living in poverty-concentrated areas, while the majority of public housing white tenants—both families and the elderly—are living in neighborhoods with substantially lower poverty rates.[9]

As of 1996, public housing was overwhelmingly minority, comprising sixty-eight percent of its population. The median household income of residents in public housing was $6,420. Although only forty-nine percent of the population in public housing was families with children, almost eighty percent of that population was consisted of single-parent families. A mere twenty-one percent of all people in public housing received a majority of their income from earned wages.[10]

The changes were frightening and discouraging for those who witnessed the crumbling of community and family, which had provided security and civility for so many years. Some packed up and left. Others stayed to fight another day. Neighborhoods that had exhibited mainstream behavior during the 1940s, 1950s, and 1960s were all of a sudden caught in a web of uncertainty. Residents who lived in or near public housing before the instability took hold, and after virtual chaos came to reign, witnessed a truly remarkable change in the function of public housing and in their neighborhoods.

Resident Experiences

Our search for reports of the change in public housing residents prompted us to interview some of the residents themselves. The people who had lived through the policy change that allowed the poorest of the poor to concentrate in public housing can best explain the impact of this policy.

Laverne Wagner, an employee of the Pittsburgh Housing Authority and a former resident of public housing recalled the pleasant, communal atmosphere of the late 1960s and early 1970s. "A lot of people took pride in where they lived. They treated it like they owned their own home." There were mothers and fathers, as well as extended families. Ms. Wagner's neighborhood was home to a lot of working families. "I remember going outside to play in my neighborhood, swimming in the swimming pool. I never had to experience any of the violence that goes on now."

One resident of Lexington Terrace Poe homes in Baltimore, Maryland entered public housing during its decline:

> I moved into public housing in 1980 . . . . Like everybody else, I wasn't going to move into public housing, because I was working and I had two jobs. But I got sick and had a heart attack. I looked around at the place I moved in, and it was roach infested, and everyone was the same color . . . . They [people living in public housing] became accustomed to living like housing was allowing them to live.

By the time this resident moved to public housing in Baltimore, the impact of federal and local changes in the criteria for the admission of families had been in place for more than a decade. A high percentage of the residents were single-parent families whose primary income was from welfare. The housing authority's staff was immersed in responding to what seemed to be constant calls for emergency service. Plumbing was often clogged; fires were frequent and caused extensive damage; and entrance keys were often lost. Resident disputes were unending and required desperate arbitration efforts by the management staff.

During the first years of her life in public housing, this tenant saw many cases of authority "neglect." The most notable, she recalled, was during a Christmas season in the early 1980s, when a number of the apartments in her complex were flooded. Decorations and presents were ruined. Yet the authority did not respond until she took action. On Christmas Eve, she brought in a news camera crew to record the damage that had occurred, thus showing the level of respect afforded residents. By the next morning, the residents with damaged possessions had been compensated.

Deirdre Salmon of Flaghouse Courts, in Baltimore, Maryland is one of those people who witnessed the tremendous change in public housing. Ms. Salmon moved into a public housing unit of her own in 1968, when she was nineteen years old. She recalled going through a fairly rigorous process, which made her feel as though she was screened by the FBI. The Housing Authority staff visited once a month to ensure that residents maintained their homes and were not disruptive to the community. There were floor captains in every building who were assigned the tasks of running meetings and maintaining order.

Ms. Salmon raised a family in Flaghouse Courts and eventually became deeply troubled by what she saw happening to her community.

Violence touched her life twice, when her husband and nephew were killed. Her husband was murdered in Lafayette Courts, another public housing project. Her nephew was killed in a stairwell just below her apartment. She knew that her losses were only part of the tragic drama that was unfolding at Flaghouse.

Much of the trouble and violence that of which Ms. Salmon became aware in the 1980s was a side effect of the drug trade. Drugs made public housing a horrible place to live Flaghouse, which is located next to the Little Italy section of Baltimore, was a frequent thoroughfare for criminals who were trying to escape the police. Often people ran into her building to escape detection. Public housing became a hideout for criminals.

Ms. Salmon's neighbors were terribly afraid of the drug dealers and their clients. It seemed that these criminals were willing to do almost anything to intimidate residents and show them who was in charge. Residents began to feel as though they were trapped in their own homes. Flaghouse, a high rise, seemed like a prison with its turnstiles and cheerless appearance. It was a depressing atmosphere over which residents felt like they had no control.

Then there came the promises of security. First came the Nation of Islam, which, according to Ms. Salmon, did an excellent job at reducing the number of disturbances. The Nation of Islam, however, was accused of trying to convert residents and was soon removed from its security duties. The Baltimore Housing Authority then hired a well-known security company. In spite of the best efforts of the new company, crime returned to its previous level. During the tenure of this particular firm, a nine-year old child was raped and murdered in Ms. Salmon's building. Though neighbors heard the cries for help, no one called security.

Tenants felt that the police were less than supportive in times of need. The Baltimore City Police were extremely reluctant to even come to public housing. Ms. Salmon stated that they generally would not respond when called unless there was gunfire. Even when they did come, the police often waited in their squad cars for several cars of back up before they would go into the building. If the elevators did not work, they would not even attempt to go upstairs.

The problems, said Ms. Salmon were not originally perpetrated by tenants of public housing. However, with the change in the screening process, she said, the housing authority admitted a population of people who were ill-equipped to handle the pressure of public housing. The drugs and violence that entered were only tolerated because a large portion of the population that lived in public housing was not able to defend itself against it.

"Moving in here was like moving in heaven," stated a long-time resident of Allequippa Terrace in Pittsburgh, Pennsylvania. Located in the Oakland section of Pittsburgh, Allequippa was built to house war workers and became one of the largest public housing projects in the Allegheny region.

"You didn't come in without a job," she said. Both she and her husband worked to provide for their family and pay the rent. Only once during her working years was this resident on public assistance.

She never imagined that she would live for more than forty years in the same public housing project, but she remembered the close relationships of neighbors, the care for the community, and the swell of positive feeling that manifested itself in a high-level of community order.

"We were all poor," she stated, but that did not preclude her from becoming close with her neighbors. Most people did not enter the system with a wealth of family and friends. Nuclear families were normal, but extended families were not. Neighbors became close, "almost like family." They met outside daily on their front porches to discuss everyday issues from their children to politics.

She also witnessed the effects of changing admission standards that has created a crumbled community and left Allequippa without a strong base of leadership or a sense of social order. Allequippa is not the same as it used to be: "I refuse to stay here without flowers," she said. "I have flowers and grass out there every year." Each year she asks neighborhood children to help her with her ritual. She has tried to maintain a level of control to keep out the confusion of drugs and violence that plagues so much of her community.

"This is [my] Court . . . . I've had some people that didn't want to move into [my] Court," she said with a smile. At the time of the interview, she was preparing to leave Allequippa to move to a project for the elderly.

"I am tired of the community," she said with some dismay. "With the change in people and everything, it's time to go." It seems that nobody really cares about the community anymore. Children run around undisciplined and unwilling to listen to their elders.

"I feel sorry for the young people. They're pressured." At a young age, she stated, children in public housing are being exposed to drugs and violence that change their perceptions.

"It's not completely housing's fault," she said in reference to the change in population. "You have these different organizations that have come up with this thing about people's rights." Although at one time neighbors had control over their neighborhoods and had the ability to have their complaints about others heard by the Housing Authority, outside organizations claiming to represent the interests of the people have gained power and forced the communities to accept any level of behavior.

It is not simply the fact that many people with serious troubles have become a part of her community that concerned her. She was worried that the human service programs no longer see their role as helping the poor become independent. Instead, they seem to assume that the problems of the poor are permanent and that making the poor comfortable is their central mission. She recalled receiving aid, when she was younger, from the Reconstruction Finance Corporation, an institution that required its clients to work while they received their benefits. Now, she stated, young women talk about "having a baby, getting on welfare, and getting a project." She complained that the structure of welfare and the nature of public housing have prevented the development of a work ethic in young people.

Notes

1. Population Reference Bureau, *A New Look at Poverty in America,* *Washington, DC: Population Reference Bureau, 1998*), 1–2.
2. US Department of Housing and Urban Development, *1979 Statistical Yearbook* (Washington, DC: Government Printing Office, 1980), pp.208–209 (Tables 66, 67), 277 (Table 6)
3. Craig Flournoy and George Rodrigue, "Separate and Unequal, Illegal segregation Pervades Nation's Subsidized Housing," *The Dallas Morning News,* 10 February 1985, 1.
4. *Ibid.*
5. *Ibid.*
6. *Ibid.*
7. Department of Housing and Urban Development, *1989 Statistical Yearbook* (Washington, DC: Government Printing Office, 1989).
8. John Goering, Ali Kamely, and Todd Richardson, *The Location and Racial Composition of Public Housing in the US: An Analysis of Racial Occupancy and Location of Public Housing Developments* (Washington, DC: HUD Office of Policy Development and Research, 1994), 1.
9. *Ibid.*
10. Department of Housing and Urban Development, *Urban Policy Brief, Promoting Self Sufficiency in Public Housing* (Washington, DC: HUD, 1996).

Chapter 10

Crime and Education

The proliferation of crime in the 1980s and early 1990s and the responses that our society has made to it are significantly related to the isolation of large numbers of impoverished people. Millions of people died or were imprisoned as a result of this increased crime, which was heavily associated with public housing.

Major increases in crime during the past three decades have been centered in areas of large cities where federally subsidized housing is located. Though we have been warned that the separation of the rich from the poor leads to increased incivility, we have chosen to disregard such warnings. We cling to the belief that each citizen is solely responsible for his behavior no matter how brutal his environment.

The Proliferation of Crime

There is a perception that minorities, particularly African Americans, are the main perpetrators of crime. They are the drug dealers, murderers, and rapists that haunt the minds of the fearful. It is an image built upon years of conditioning. Out of a complex web of images displayed by the media and long-standing doctrines that are perpetually spouted by popular figures, including politicians and academics, there has emerged a fear for urban crime. It is the adjective *urban* that is of particular interest, for urban crime is the type of crime perpetually discussed and examined. The concept of urban crime that consists of distinct racial and socioeconomic traits is important to understanding why particular strategies have been employed to rectify the situation.

There are indeed high levels of crime in urban areas. The murder and violent crime rates for cities, though on a recent downturn, were especially high during the 1980s and early 1990s and have helped to establish the fear of urban violence. The rate of killing in impoverished areas reached such a high level that entire cities were shaped by the phenomenon. More specifically, the fact that such violence was perpetrated primarily by minorities caused a tremendous backlash and increasing hostility toward the neighborhoods in which such crime occurred.

Surprisingly, however, murder rates almost seventy years ago were higher than today. The Great Depressionand its dire economic times surely provoked despair and frustration and led to increased tumult. At its peak, during the 1930s, the murder rate was 9.7 per 100,000. After World War II, murder rates dropped precipitously, to a low of 4.5 per 100,000 in the 1950s. Then in the 1960s, there was a steady rise that continued through the 1970s and reached a peak of 10.7 per 100,000 in 1980. The 1980s hosted a mild, yet short-lived decline. In the early 1990s, serious concern arose once again over the increasing rate, which again surpassed 10 per 100,000 for several years in a row. Since then, it has declined. However, the most startling aspect of the murder rate is that African Americans are six times more likely to be the victims of murder than whites and seven times as likely to commit murder.[1]

The proliferation of gang violence in the 1980s played a tremendous role in the increases in murder rates. Since 1976, gang-related violence has increased fivefold. In the past twenty-five years, most of the murders, particularly those associated with gang activity, have taken place in large cities. More than one-quarter of all murders since 1976 have taken place in cities of one million or more, and more than half of all murders have taken place in cities of one hundred thousand or more.[2]

To understand the significance of the association of minority crime with concentrated urban impoverishment is to recognize the impact of public and subsidized housing upon the consideration of crime. It is within areas of concentrated poverty, where public and subsidized housing is concentrated, that violence and crime have been most intense. The perpetually lower standards for admission to subsidized housing resulted in the creation of areas with disorders of unprecedented intensity. Influenced by the cultural norms of American society and lacking the support of stable families and community, some impoverished areas have developed unusual sets of standards.

Although many people may acknowledge some difference between the resources available to those who live in impoverished areas and those who do not, a point of extreme contention is the ability and the morality of the individual resident. Participation in crime is viewed by many to be a personal choice. Ultimately, the decision to commit a crime is up to the individual. Many contend that there are alternatives to criminal activity. Success stories from impoverished urban areas are often cited to prove the ability of the individual to transcend the corruptive surroundings. The strength of the individual predisposes that person to success or failure. If one can be influenced by surroundings to such an extent as to be induced to violate established laws, then that person is deemed weak. Such a person is not guided by a moral compass that would lead to a path of righteousness and good deeds (though the definition of righteousness is certainly debatable). It is this reliance on individual character that dictates much of the way in which we deal with crime.

Responses to Crime

The world outside of impoverished areas is the world that controls the system that deals with antisocial behavior. As has been tradition for centuries, the typical way to deal with criminal activity is with punishment. After a crime has been committed, the offender is embedded into a system to exact retribution for the committed offense. It has seemed like a logical and practical way to deal with the criminal.

What has defined the nature of response to urban problems is the idea of difference. The difference between the criminally minded and the rest of the population is the focus of explanations surrounding crime. Misdeeds, particularly in urban areas, are seen as the expressions of immorality. Neither the environmental norms are nor the structure that facilitates such misdeeds matter. Criminal activity, however it is defined, requires punishment.

Over the last forty years, the burgeoning consideration of crime has led to discussions of the necessary responses. As crime has become a topic of increasing social relevance, it has taken on great political importance. Elected and appointed officials at all levels of government have been forced to show that they will be tough on crime. In an effort to show their commitment to morality, many politicians have come to support extreme punishment. There are constant battles to show who is tougher on crime and who is the most committed to ensuring the safety of the "good public" and locking up the "bad criminals." "Tough guys" are those who have shown their willingness to sweep away the "immoral" for the greater good of the world.

Being tough on the people who commit crimes has required the perpetual strengthening of the criminal justice system. Police, the courts, and prisons have become an integral social force as a result.

Perhaps most notable is the increase in funding that has been granted to enforce the laws. In 1948, the per capita expenditure on police protection was $3.48 (both figures in 1967 dollars). By 1978, that figure had reached $91.58. Overall law enforcement expenditures have been almost as staggering. In 1982, thirty-five billion dollars were spent on the system. By 1994, that figure had risen to $103.5 billion and since has only increased. The increased expenditures money have been funneled into several areas, including prison construction, increased numbers of police, increased prosecutors, and increased executions. In five years, between 1990 and 1995, 213 new correctional facilities were built.[3]

Incarceration

Increased incarceration has given birth to a steadily growing industry. One in twenty people will go to jail during their lifetime. The rate of incarceration is almost 500 per 100,000. State and federal prison populations doubled between 1987 and 1997. Even more disturbing than the sheer number of people incarcerated is the fact that prisons are increasingly populated by minorities. By 1996, sixty-three percent of jail inmates were racial or ethnic minorities. Twenty-eight percent of black males will go to prison during their lifetime.

The incredible rate of incarceration among African Americans has come under scrutiny in recent years, according to several studies. Both blacks and Hispanics have been found to be treated more harshly than whites by the justice system at all levels. Blacks and Hispanics are more likely than whites to be arrested, held in jail, sent to trial, convicted, and sent to prison for longer periods of time. Black youths without a record are six times as likely as whites to be sent to prison, nine times as likely to be sent to prison for committing a violent offense, and forty-eight times as likely for a drug offense as whites who have committed similar acts.[4]

The increasing severity of punishment has been seen as a way to deter criminals from committing certain acts. The creation of harsher laws was intended, supposedly, as a preventive measure. However, these laws have not effectively prevented imprisonment. "Three strikes" laws and codes compelling mandatory minimums have sent more and more people away for longer and longer periods of time.

In particular, harsh laws have affected urban areas. Many of the people who have been punished as a result of increasingly severe laws have come from primarily poor, urban, minority areas.

Large urban areas are often the largest contributors to the state prison population. Los Angeles County, for example, has but twelve percent of the population of the state of California, yet provided thirty-seven percent of the state prison population. Baltimore City, home to fifteen percent of the population in the state of Maryland, provided fifty percent of the prison population. Cook County, Illinois (Chicago) provided sixty-nine of the state prison population.[5]

Chicago, Baltimore, and Los Angeles are, coincidentally, cities with three of the largest historically troubled public housing authorities in the country. These cities are known to have very large concentrations of impoverished people.

Drug-related Crime

Years ago, drug dealers were generally older men who avoided children and sold discreetly. The vision of the drug market now, however, is entirely different. In the 1980s, the proliferation of crack cocaine became tightly bound with the image of impoverished African American urban communities. More important, the distributors and users were increasingly young. With this drug came an unprecedented level of violence and crime. The fear of such drug-related crime caused the shift in the way we considered drugs. The criminal element that was a part of the drug underworld was not at all a part of mainstream society. The unconventional methods employed both to obtain and to distribute drugs surprised many people. Poor minority areas quickly became a part of a system that would come to control virtually every aspect of their lives. Though drugs would eventually become known in other, wealthier environments, the most impoverished areas became the haven for the dealers and the violence that accompanied them. The reaction to the proliferation of drug-related activity was to increase the punishment for those who committed those crimes. The number of people in state prison for drug-related crimes, such as possession and distribution, increased by eightfold between 1969 and 1991 as a result of these laws and their intense implementation. In 1996, fifty-eight percent of the federal prison population and twenty-one percent of state prisoners were behind bars for nonviolent, drug-related offenses.[6]

Almost eighty percent of the people behind bars for drug abuse violations in 1997 were arrested for possession.

Yet the simple distribution and consumption of illegal drugs was not the only crime associated with narcotics. A study by the National Center on Addiction and Substance Abuse at Columbia University estimated that eighty percent of those in jail or prison were "seriously involved" with substance abuse, meaning that they

> . . . have used an illegal drug regularly, been incarcerated for drugs, DUI, [were] under [the] influence of alcohol or drugs when committing a crime, committed an offense for drug money, or have a history of drug and alcohol abuse.[7]

The increase in drug-related budgetary matters has been dramatic. In fiscal year 1981, this country spent $1.5 billion on the budget to combat illegal drugs. By fiscal year 1999, that figure had risen to $17.89 billion, almost half of which was spent on the justice system.[8] Treatment for substance abuse has never been a priority for government. Though each dollar spent on treatment saves nearly seven dollars on law enforcement, the war on drugs continues to be a significant part of federal policy. Consistently, the seizure of illegal substances in mass amounts is touted as a success. Yet the market for drugs does not diminish merely because a small supply disappears.

Police Experience

As crime became more intense in public housing, some housing authorities were driven to establish police units exclusively for their developments.

One major public housing police department has drug-sniffing dogs, computers and cameras in the squad cars, transport vehicles, a traffic unit. In our interview, an official of the department discussed the fact that his is the only accredited police department in the entire city. The annual budget, is about five million dollars. There are eighty officers, who are a part of a twenty-four-hour service.

"The housing police department was established probably twenty-five years ago to supplement the city because the baseline services force was basically not happening in public housing," stated one high ranking official in the department. He continued,

Four years ago there was a consultant company that came in and did a survey on what residents of public housing thought [was] their greatest need. And their very first thing on the list was safety. It wasn't about rent. It wasn't about food. It was about safety. They didn't feel safe walking out of their apartments.

The residents of public housing expressed in no uncertain terms the dominance of criminal activity in their neighborhoods. The response of the housing authority was to create a police force of a superior caliber to respond more specifically to the needs of residents.

If you were a criminal, you went to public housing because somebody took care of you. You didn't have police forces out there. You didn't have the backing of the surrounding community saying, you know we've gotta do something.

Without the backing of the community to fight the infiltration of crime, public housing succumbed to the pressure of the streets.

Often, it was not the residents of public housing, who were the perpetrators of crime but outsiders. "It's not the residents; it's all of the people coming into [public housing]," the official stated . . . . Public housing often acts as a magnetic force to attract disturbance and antisocial behavior. Those who recognize the severe problems of people living in public housing often take advantage of their fragile state.

As police methods become more attuned to the ways of the street, criminals have responded with increasingly sophisticated techniques:

As we buy new equipment, they find some way to get around the new equipment. The drug traffickers have moved from the street corners to houses, where they have their radio systems. They have their watchers. They have an Internet system. They know when you leave the station. When you're making five thousand dollars a day and you're a mid-level dealer, you have to know where the police are.

The official described an ever-present battle between the police and the dealers, who are sometimes revered within public housing communities for their cunning and ingenuity.

Though drug-related crime is still a significant source of the problems within public housing,

The biggest disturbance we have here is domestic violence. By far. It has taken over right now, and I can't answer why. It's not just the husband beating the wife, it's the wife beating the husband, or the child beating the father and mother.

The fundamental relationships that exist in most families, regardless of structure, are often lacking within families in public housing. As a result, the police have become interim counselors, settling disputes between arguing family members.

Traditional family life is no longer a force in public housing. The official described a typical public-housing household in his city:

> Single women with 2.5 children. You know, [men] under the age of 25. They're staying illegally in the apartments because they're not on the lease. Most of them who come in are transit guys. They'll be there maybe for a couple of weeks and then leave. There's no family here. There's no husbands and wives and kids all raised together . . . . There's no family groups where you can have family values, where there's a figure they can look up to. There's no mentors for the kids. The mentors for the kids are the drug dealers.

If we look back forty years, we find that the vast majority of families with children in public housing were two-parent families. Now, however, there are consistent patterns of transient relationships.

The official thought he knew why the atmosphere of public housing has changed so much in the past twenty years.

> I think management didn't care who moved in anymore. I think values broke down. People started moving out [and the Authority said], let's bring in whoever. We've got poor people; let's just move 'em in. We'll put them in a tall high-rise, and that's where they're going to live for the rest of their lives.

Though the official is proud of his effort to improve the police department of the housing authority, he acknowledged that he and his staff are not the solution to the problem:

> You've gotta educate them, you've gotta get them to go back to school, want to do better for themselves. Public housing should be a stepping stone to where you get money to put away so you can buy a house, and you can live in a nice neighborhood, and send your kids to nice schools and college, and they get a job and they go on and on.

Public housing in and of itself must change in accordance with the residents of the communities so as to reconfigure the very nature of housing and hope for the poor. Cyclical battles with drug dealers cannot be won by force alone, as long as such activity is the most effective means by which to obtain material satisfaction.

Urban Public Education

The deterioration of urban education also can be attributed, in part, to the concentration of poverty. Areas where public housing is centered are also the areas where school failures are most often found. However, our responses have been centered on changing schools, giving school choice, providing vouchers, and holding schools accountable for their students. Urban schools (teachers, principals, and other administrators), however, cannot alone be blamed for their failure. They have been burdened by the pressure of servicing vast numbers of students with very serious problems.

Public education, in most major cities, does not live up to the standards that characterized its work in the early years of our nation. Test scores are low, teachers are not well paid, and drop-out rates are astonishingly high. Repeated efforts to solve to this problem with urban education include vouchers to send children to private schools, changing school leadership, and the creation of charter schools.

Most of us know that education is not limited to the classroom. It extends to the home, church, extracurricular activities, and a host of other points of experience where children learn informally.

Numerous studies have been undertaken to examine the breadth of the failure of urban education. The young people who attend city schools are far more likely to live in poverty than their suburban counterparts (though children in rural areas still have a higher chance of living in poverty than either).[9] Children who live in poverty are very likely to come from families with parents who have low levels of education. Education levels of parents have been linked to their children's educational achievement. Children who attend schools where there is concentrated poverty are less likely to have the family structure and economic security and stability that are most associated with desirable educational outcomes, and are more likely to be exposed to safety and health risks that place their well being in jeopardy.[10] They are also less likely to have access to regular health care. Thus, the urban student often begins school with serious disadvantages that can include material and health deficiencies, as well as an environment that does not value traditional education.

Extremely poor school-wide academic performance has been traced to schools that service severely impoverished communities.[11] As the proportion of poor students increases, student performance on achievement tests goes down.[12] Young people who attend these schools are far more likely to drop out than their counterparts at schools where the poor are not concentrated. The educational achievement of individual students is strongly associated with the educational background of other students who attend the same school.[13] People who attend high-poverty schools are more likely than people who attend other schools to be living in poverty later in life than others, mostly because of higher rates of unemployment.[14]

Schools in which there is a high level of poverty often have significantly more disciplinary problems than other schools. As a result of disciplinary problems and the low wages, urban impoverished schools often have a very difficult time hiring and retaining top quality teachers.[15]

The emphasis placed on traditional education in the home is important in determining whether a child will have strong support in the traditional academic setting. Children who come from families where there is a low value placed upon traditional education are at a disadvantage when they enter school. Even after they enter school, lack of parental nurture and support can contribute to poor performance. According to the Urban Institute, students who attend severely impoverished schools are less likely to discuss their education with their parents than are other students.[16]

In communities with successful schools, particularly successful public schools, an active role for parents is essential. Schools that have extensive academic and extracurricular programs are often the same schools that have strong Parent-Teacher Associations. Students at schools that serve severely impoverished areas are less likely to participate in school-sponsored activities. Often, the reason for this lack of involvement is a lack of available activities.[17]

It is not difficult to trace the impact of the problems of schools from classrooms to principals to superintendents to school boards. All, ultimately, are seen as having failed to meet the standards of learning the city had set for itself, but they cannot, alone, be held responsible.

Indeed, there seems to be a correlation between concentrated poverty and serious urban problems even beyond crime and education. More research and study must be conducted into the impact of concentrated poverty and what government can do to help resolve the resulting problems. As these problems have proliferated, however, people in suffering communities have struggled to retain their hopes and dreams. There are programs that work to improve areas of concentrated poverty even against great odds.

Notes

1. National Center for Health Statistics, Vital Statistics, Hyattsville, MD. Health Center for Health Statistics, Data Division, NCHS Web site, http://www.cdc.gov/nchs/products/pubs/pubd/nvsr/nvsr.htm

2. *Ibid.*

3. Bureau of Justice Statistics, *Sourcebook of Criminal Justice Statistics.* (Washington, DC Bureau of Justice Statistics), http://www.ojp.usdoj .gov/bjs/abstract/csfcf95.htm.

4. Michael A. Fletcher, "Criminal Justice Disparities Cited: Blacks, Hispanics Treated More Harshly at Every Stage," *The Washington Post*, 4 April 2000, A2.

5. William J. Sabol, *Crime Control and Common Sense Assumptions Underlying the Expansion of the Prison Population* (Urban Institute website, http://www.urban.org/ Template.cfm?Section=ByAuthor&NavMenuID=63& template=/TaggedContent/ViewPublication.cfm&PublicationID=5922

6. William J. Sabol and James P. Lynch, *Crime Policy Report: Did Getting Tough on Crime Pay?*, Urban Institute Web site, 1997. http://www.urban.org/Template.cfm?Section=ByAuthor& NavMenuID=63& template=/TaggedContent/ViewPublication.cfm&PublicationID=5922

7. Steve Belenko, *Behind Bars: Substance Abuse and America's Prison Population* (New York: Columbia University National Center on Addiction and Substance Abuse, 1998), 2.

8. Bureau of Justice Statistics, *Sourcebook of Criminal Justice Statistics.* (Washington, DC: Bureau of Justice Statistics, 1998), http://www.ojp.usdoj.gov/bjs/dcf/dcb.htm

9. National Center for Education Statistics, Executive Summary in *Urban Schools*, (Washington, DC: US Dept. of Education, 1996), v.

10. *Ibid.*, vi.

11. *Ibid.*, v.

12. *Ibid.*, 20.

13. *Ibid.*, 31.

14. *Ibid.*, 20.

15. *Ibid.*, viii.

16. *Ibid.*, v.

17. *Ibid.*

Chapter 11

Changes in Washington, DC

By the 1980s, the Anacostia/Congress Heights area of Washington, DC was best known for its high crime rate, high level of disease and illnesses, large number of single-parent families, high rate of unemployment and welfare, and unprecedented levels of school drop outs. Block after block of the three-story garden type apartments built following World War II were vacant. Many of the vacant apartments were plundered by drug dealers and users. As a result, fearful residents moved, most of them bound for adjacent Prince Georges County, Maryland.

Most of the remaining residents in the area were in public housing and privately owned subsidized housing, but even subsidized housing was hard to fill. Many people were intimidated by the social environment and refused to accept vacant subsidized dwellings in Far Southeast Washington.

By the mid-1980s there were ten thousand vacant apartments in Anacostia/Congress Heights. As apartments became vacant, landlords became desperate. Some of the private owners applied for and received subsidies to attract lower-income families. By the late 1980s, there were, in one section of Anacostia, more than twenty thousand subsidized dwellings, both publicly and privately owned.

Government services did not seem to work. More policemen were in Anacostia, but crime continued unabated. Schools made special efforts to deal with increasing difficulty with students. Many studies were undertaken. None of the changes seemed to be effective.

Turning Around a Community

In about 1985, I was invited to discuss the social and economic issues in Anacostia with a group of concerned citizens. This meeting led me to participate in the formation of the Anacostia Coordinating Council (ACC). At the time, I was the chairman of the Southeast Community House, which was a settlement house. People went there for recreation and to talk about their problems.

The ACC, a group of business and civic leaders, was organized in an effort to halt the social and economic deterioration of the area. One of its first efforts was to persuade the mayor and leaders of the metropolitan area's subway system to extend it to Anacostia in accordance with a plan that have been approved previously by the city. Construction of the Anacostia subway station had been delayed because leaders in adjacent Prince Georges County were not able to agree on the preferred route for the subway system as it entered the county from Anacostia. Response from the mayor and other officials was timely and the new Anacostia subway station was approved for construction.

With the assistance of a professor of city planning from The George Washington University, Dorn McGrath, and his associate, Margaret K. O'Bryon, the ACC undertook a study of Historic Anacostia. The study was prompted by reports that some of the historic buildings in the area were in a state of serious neglect. Under the aegis of the ACC, a group of students from nearby Kramer Junior High School were trained to observe housing deterioration and, under close supervision, performed the survey.

The ACC developed a plan based on the findings of the survey to encourage owners to restore dilapidated historic buildings. Though some dilapidation remains, many owners have brought their properties up to code. Others are currently in the process of improving their buildings.

One afternoon in June of 1988 as I left an afternoon meeting at the Greater Southeast Hospital where I served on the Board of Directors, I passed two nearby public playgrounds where the baseball fields were empty. Schools had been closed for several weeks and the playgrounds were adjacent to public housing developments and several privately owned subsidized developments. Something within me suggested that I make a survey of other playgrounds to see just how widespread the nonuse of public recreation areas had become. After all, this was the Wward with the largest number of children in the city.

I visited thirteen playgrounds and found no one on them. Puzzled and curious, I called the director of the city's Department of Recreation to ask why the fields were not in use. The director felt that the youngsters in this area simply had little interest in baseball. I asked whether he would help if I could organize some teams of young people to participate in a baseball league. He agreed enthusiastically.

Within two weeks we had organized ten teams with fifteen members each. We recruited coaches from the area and solicited contributions from local businesses for gloves and other equipment. After several weeks of regular team competition, I noticed a trend. When practice was called for 4:00 P.M., the team members showed up at 2:00 P.M. When the games were over at 7:30, the team members were not eager to go home.

The young people playing were mostly boys between twelve and sixteen years of age. Team members seemed to enjoy the attention they received, the regularity and order of team play, and the care and direction given by coaches and supporters. In this area where juvenile delinquency and crime were at the highest levels in the city, there seemed to be a hunger among the team members for a role to play, a reliable setting, and responsive adults.

Anacostia/Congress Heights Partnership

At the same time, I was a participant in a city-wide effort to help the homeless. Working with Oliver T. Carr, the civic-minded owner of the city's largest real estate development firm, who cochaired the coalition appointed to develop the city's response to homelessness, we developed a plan that called for the formation of a partnership between government, business, and private human service leaders to address the issue. Since I'd been working in Anacostia with theACC and knew that many of the homeless people were coming from that area, I decided it might be appropriate for us to have a neighborhood partnership as well.

I joined Far Southeast leaders in forming the Anacostia/Congress Heights Partnership for the Prevention of Homelessness. The Board of Directors of the new partnership was drawn from resident leaders and representatives of public and private organizations serving the area. We did not want the Partnership to be a permanent fixture in the community. We wanted to help residents do things for themselves.

The first thing I noticed when we began the new Partnership was that there was no sense of community in many parts of Anacostia, particularly those with large tracts of subsidized housing. People didn't speak to each other. Very few residents smiled at each other when they met on the street. There were no organizations of any strength except a few churches, and most of the poorest of the poor did not attend church.

Our plan was to find families who were at risk of becoming homeless and help them either to stay where they were or to find other quarters in the neighborhood. Most of the people who had become homeless had come from public housing. Many homeless families had been evicted for failure to pay rent, or they had failed to live up to other responsibilities in their leases. The Partnership decided that the most important need in the neighborhood was the renewal of a sense of community. We called the supplementary efforts community-building. *We wanted to identify potential leaders, arrange for neighbors to meet to discuss common concerns, and eventually take action to eliminate the problems of their community.*

After selecting Brenda Richardson, a licensed social worker, as executive director of the Partnership, and with the help of Margaret K. O'Bryon, a consultant/volunteer from The George Washington University, we agreed that our homeless prevention program would begin at a nearby public housing project called Sheridan Terrace. This development of approximately three hundred dwellings was a combination of town houses and garden-type apartments. We decided that the best course of action would be to discuss the homeless problem with a group of residents. Ms. Richardson and a founding member, Hannah Hawkins of the Board of Directors of the Partnership, met with them. They found that child neglect was a pressing and immediate problem.

Children's Center

Partnership leaders, board, and staff decided that addressing the child neglect problem could lead to a better understanding of the potential for homelessness among residents. Accordingly, we decided to establish a children's center that would provide an after-school program for latch-key kids and other children from Sheridan Terrace. The center offered help with homework and provided snacks, conversation, and indoor games.

One of the effects of the children's center was that parents became more involved with each other: they began to depend on each other, look at each other, and even complain about each other. They began to communicate. We brought in some volunteers to help parents prepare food for the children in the evening, play games with the children, and to talk to the parents about the problems the children were having. That kind of interaction began to grow as people felt comfortable with each other.

Hannah Hawkins, a local resident, became the director of the center. Her program became so popular that she decided she wanted to move to a larger place over on Morris Road in a site where the Southeast Neighborhood House had been located. When she moved, the women in Sheridan Terrace decided they didn't want to send their children over to Morris Road. They wanted to continue their own program. We asked who was going to run it. They named Mrs. Myrtle Loughry, a resident. We accepted their nomination and acquainted her with the space and equipment available and the lists of children and parents who had been active in the program.

The program became so successful that, again, there was not enough space to accommodate all of the children. So the Children's Center moved to Macedonia Baptist Church, just one block from the Sheridan Terrace Public Housing Development. She stayed there for a year or two. Mrs. Loughry moved again after the program outgrew that space. She moved to the community room at the nearby Washington View Apartments and then to Wilkinson Elementary School. When she outgrew that space, she moved to Douglass Junior High School. After more than eight years, Mrs. Loughry became the director of the neighborhood Boys and Girls Club of America.

Meanwhile, Hannah Hawkins had established her child care program, named "Children of Mine" on Morris Road. Her determination, commitment, and sagacity produced phenomenal success in attracting the support of volunteers and donors and the cooperation of the parents of many children. Her program continues to serve the community.

Both Mrs. Hawkins and Mrs. Loughry played significant roles in the ultimate restoration of a stable and civil environment in Far Southeast Washington.

Established Neighborhood Institutions

As the Partnership's work spread throughout the area, it became clear that many churches were already engaged in efforts to help the needy families in the area. As in many communities, churches contribute greatly to the lives of children throughout Anacostia.

Though many of the members of churches in the Far Southeast area had moved to the suburbs or other areas of the city, they were ready, willing, and able to assist the families who lived close to their churches. As residents began to assume more leadership in the community, they encouraged their neighbors to be responsive to the helping hands at nearby churches. Gradually the interaction between churches in Anacostia and their neighbors increased and it was evident that the faith community was a reliable source of help for all residents.

Adjacent to the Sheridan Terrace development was the Bethlehem Baptist Church, which, for some years, had operated a day care center for working mothers. When the day care center at Sheridan Terrace moved, some resident families sought care for their children at Bethlehem. The Bethlehem children's program was run by a retired school teacher. She arranged a cooperative relationship with the nearby Savoy Elementary School program. Bethlehem children participated in reading programs and tours of museums and other cultural centers. Students were required to write brief reports of their experiences. The combination of public and after-school programs generated increased parental participation and improved student performances.

Allen AME Church on Alabama Avenue, close to the Woodland Terrace Public Housing Project, engaged a retired recreation department worker to provide special help to children who were caught up in disorderly, sometimes criminal behavior and failing in school. The church's facilities were also offered to community groups for organizational meetings.

Macedonia Baptist Church continued its commitment to the residents of Sheridan Terrace Public Housing Development. Individual mothers in the development were encouraged to send their children to Sunday school at Macedonia. Some enterprising members began to prepare Thanksgiving celebrations where residents of Sheridan Terrace joined members of Macedonia in enjoying this special day.

Young's Memorial Church of Christ Holiness, which served the same neighborhood as Allen AME Church, also established day care facilities for working mothers and a food distribution center for the needy and recruited volunteers from among its members to aid neighboring residents who were experiencing great difficulties. The minister, Reverend Herbert Chambers, a member of the Board of Directors of the Anacostia/Congress Heights Partnership, recently reported a substantial increase in the number of young residents of the area who were attending his church.

Eventually in the Far Southeast area there were more than ten after-school programs run by residents. Directors of the centers sought ideas and help from each other as they came to meetings sponsored by the Anacostia/Congress Heights Partnership.

We were most fortunate that our consultant at the Partnership, Margaret K. O'Bryon, was also the daughter of the Minister of the Lutheran Church of the Reformation, which is located on Capitol Hill, only a block from the US Supreme Court. An assistant minister from that church, Pastor Wanda McNeill, came to inform me that Reverend Keller, the senior minister, had offered her services to our Southeast effort. Building on earlier experiences with the baseball teams, I asked whether she would consider making an effort to get the youth to return to the ball fields and playgrounds. She readily accepted the challenge and within a week suggested a plan to organize baseball competition. When winter came, she planned to expand the program with opportunities for basketball competition. The program, under the aegis of what is now called the Southeast Ministry, has continued over the last decade to restore interest and enthusiasm among children and their parents in participating in recreational activities.

Coordinating Services

In 1991, the Partnership formally decided to broaden its mission to help encourage the growth of the community. The prevention of homelessness would continue to be one of several objectives.

Many of the residents of Sheridan Terrace were "clients" of social services such as the DC Welfare Department, and Family and Child Services. Residents saw a social worker every now and then, but there was no specific plan developed for helping families work toward stability and independence. As a result, the Partnership initiated the Family Review Committee to discuss their work and develop a plan for each family.

The Partnership was fully convinced that services should be helping people become independent so that their services would no longer be needed. Handing them a check every now and then was not the answer. We had to introduce residents to new education and job opportunities, and help mothers to make sure that they took their children to the health clinic regularly. The Partnership, in cooperation with Georgetown University Hospital, brought in medical personnel to areas that were unserviced by physicians, facilitated conflict resolution *groups for young people, and held awards ceremonies to recognize the accomplishments of residents.*

The Efforts of Individuals

In addition to Mrs. Hawkins and Mrs. Loughry, my work in Anacostia allowed me to meet many people who have fought to change their community, people who really believe in the ability of people to overcome their difficult surroundings and achieve a state of independent living.

Brenda Jones

Brenda Jones has, for many years, been a community activist. Ms. Jones, with a small staff and limited funds, has tried to make a difference. Her office has always been in the Parklands development and her clients are principally from adjacent public housing developments. Her office walls are almost completely covered with notices of training opportunities, health care opportunities, job opportunities, and invitations to all civic meetings the area hosts. Ms. Jones has been a positive influence in the community, creating special programs to address the needs of residents. As one of her admirers said, "Brenda is a fearless lady."

She started the Parklands Community Center in 1980. Now the Center helps to facilitate a myriad of services and programs. "I try to provide the young people with every kind of experience that they need to grow and become productive, positive adults," said Ms. Jones. Now, several organizations under the Parklands umbrella provide activities such as job training, computer literacy, and field trips to the Smithsonian.

The community center, which is located near two of the largest public housing projects in the city, has been host to the progeny of many families affected by drugs. "The general family is where there's a drug problem and a literacy problem," she says of the families who come to her center. On the corner of Alabama Avenue and Stanton Road, just up the street from the Parklands Community, there was a drug market that had recently been shut down. "That was two months ago," she said. "After things cool down, they'll be right back up there again."

> Drug abuse is really the [cause of] a lot of the problems in the last fifteen or twenty years. I remember, I was on 21st and Mississippi

Avenue, in the mid eighties, that kids were coming into the center, who were well kept, would be in a nice household, but would deteriorate. All of a sudden, their attitude started deteriorating. And we started looking at what happened. Come to find out that the mothers would be on drugs. Drug dealers would have taken over their apartment. That was a big thing. They [drug dealers] would come in and get these girls on drugs, and take over their apartments and set up shop. And you had girls who lived for five dollars a month, to be put out for nonpayment of rent. That's how bad it was, and children [were] just devastated by what was happening to their lifestyle . . . .
I think that the problem is that we don't have any drug treatment centers. The city doesn't fund any drug treatment centers. It's a travesty, really, all of the addicts we have in the city. So many children have dead fathers, incarcerated fathers and even incarcerated mothers. That's why I try to encourage people to take a chance on themselves—to break out of this dungeon of despair.

The Family Strengthening and Support program was started in 1995 after Ms. Jones and employees at the Parklands Community Center began to explore the reasons for misbehavior and poor attitude among children who attended their program. They began to realize that the values that were being taught at the Center were not being reinforced at home. Ms. Jones realized that it was not simply children in the community who needed support, but parents, too. Many parents in the community were young. These young parents were sometimes influenced by friends and relatives who often used violence to gain their children's attention, and themselves paid little attention in return to their children.

"From the beginning, it was a struggle to get people to participate," said Dionne Kingsbury, a public housing resident and facilitator of the Family Strengthening and Support Program. She said,

A lot of organizations come into the community and say they're going to do this and that for the residents of the community. And basically, when they come in they get the money and the community doesn't see anything.

The families helped by the program are generally those in which there is either a drug or literacy problem, and sometimes both. It is no simple task to encourage people to change their ways. Sometimes two or three years pass before there is any noticeable change. If families do not respond or seem uninterested in changing their family patterns, Ms. Jones lets them go. "They'll be back when they're ready to change," she stated.

As Ms. Jones describes them, many community residents are extremely fragile and have little trust in each other, much less in so-called helpful organizations. Many people do not believe that they have the power to change their own lives, much less have an impact upon their community. Even so, more and more people are being reached.

Catherine Jackson, a long time resident of Parklands, was forced to drop out of school in the seventh grade and has been a recipient of public assistance for some time. "I just thank God for the Family Strengthening and Support Program," she said. The program has helped place her daughters in special schools and has allowed her to take a vacation with her family, something she had never been able to do previously. Ms. Jackson now has a job, which she hopes will lead to further employment opportunities. The program has also helped strengthen her reading skills, and she soon hopes to obtain her GED. Brenda Jones has been a strong influence on Far Southeast Washington, spreading the word of change for stability and human growth.

Jackie Massey

At a community meeting called by the Anacostia/Congress Heights Partnership in about 1990, Mrs. Jackie Massey stood up to describe the conditions at Valley Green. It was then a public housing project that had the worst reputation in Far Southeast. It had the reputation of being the center of crime and illnesses. Valley Green embodied all the problems that characterized the area at the time. She spoke eloquently about what she thought the community could do and should do and what she was willing to do.

Mrs. Massey thought that the problems in the community wouldn't be resolved until we were able to get the residents together. It was important to have services but those services must help people to do for themselves.

She did not begin with any complex or sophisticated programs. She did simple things, but they were effective. She got people together to talk about their problems and take some actions themselves to try to overcome them. At that time Valley Green was virtually vacant. She and six other families lived in one building.

Across the street from Valley Green was another public housing project called Highland Dwellings, and she had impact there, too. There was a program for the distribution of food. Ms. Massey arranged, with only six families, to have that program headquartered at Valley Green. People came from all around the neighborhood,

*including other public housing projects, to get food. She was the
unspoken proprietor of it.*

*Valley Green badly needed improvement, but there seemed to be
some uncertainty about how it might be done. Though most dwellings
were vacant, Mrs. Massey and her husband refused to move. They were
committed to the development, which is built on a hillside overlooking
the Oxon Run Park. Ms. Massey was convinced that conditions would
improve if the residents, the housing authority, and the community
would only work together.*

*As chairman of the Anacostia/Congress Heights Partnership, I
frequently traveled about the area to observe progress in resident
groups. One of my visits was to Valley Green, where some residents led
by Ms. Massey had decided to exercise each day. The group walked
around the block on which the development was located several times. I
was told that, although the women initiated the exercise, after several
days they were joined by men. On my visit, approximately one-fourth of
the walkers were men. Eventually the group included children as well.*

*It was not long before the group decided to change their diet as a
way to improve health and lose weight. When I first visited the vacant
apartment that the group had been granted for cooking, eating, and
office space, the women were busy cooking in the kitchen. A month or
so later when I visited, the men were cooking and the women were busy
planning activities for young people in the area.*

*As a result of her activities in Valley Green, Mrs. Massey was
recruited to be trained to help manage a senior citizens' public housing
project in another part of the city and is now employed in a
management position. She was also appointed to the Board of
Directors of the DC Housing Finance Agency, which raises mortgage
money for affordable housing through the sale of municipal bonds.
Jackie Massey, who has borne great tragedies in her life, seems to be
possessed with courage and hope of special dimensions. Her vision is
remarkable. Her participation in the rebuilding of the neighborhood
she came to fear and love is unquestionably one of the reasons it is on
the way to turning around.*

Dorothea Ferrell

Back in 1958, when Dorothea Ferrell moved into Barry Farm, the
community was

> . . . beautifully landscaped. The houses were green and white, and
> everybody had beautiful yards. The children were well behaved, and

we had different clubs in the community. We had programs for young people. We had gatherings like cookouts, where everybody participated. I feel now, that it was like a dream.

Because my husband was a veteran, we were allowed to move into Barry Farms [*sic*]. We've been here ever since. My husband and I made a pact that he would work days (he was a construction worker), and I would work evenings, so one parent would always be there with the children.

Mrs. Ferrell said that she began to notice the changes in her neighborhood in 1980 when the Barry Farm development was remodeled as a permanent public housing development. Many new families moved to the new community. Among them, said Mrs. Ferrell, were some who seemed unable to care properly for their children. The friendly neighborhood began to change as conflict within and between families increased. "I was angry," said Mrs. Ferrell. "That's one of the reasons I became active in the community."

Soon after we met in 1992, Mrs. Ferrell asked whether the Partnership could help her to obtain some sewing machines. Because she had some experience as a seamstress, she wanted to help some of the growing number of young mothers at Barry Farm to learn to sew so that they might make clothes for their children, or at least make repairs. We were successful in obtaining twenty machines. Ms. Ferrell obtained space at Barry Farm, and the training began to teach mothers to make clothing for their children.

For years the Birney School student population has been drawn primarily from the Barry Farms Public Housing Project. Several years ago the principal asked for help from the DC Mental Health Association in coping with children whose siblings or parents had been killed in one violent outburst or another.

Birney's new principal, Ms. Yvonne Morse, met with Mrs. Ferrell to get a description of life in the neighborhood and asked for help in raising the levels of achievement of these students. These students were far below the national average in test scores. With help from reading clubs, mentors, increased parent participation, and week-long work by both the principal and Ms. Ferrell, Birney School students in the year 2000 had improved test scores nearly to the national averages. Parent participation had doubled. School attendance was more regular. School drop-outs sharply decreased.

Barry Farm, where nine children were killed in drug-related shootings in 1989, is now the scene of revitalization. Welfare mothers are being trained for employment. Reading clubs have been established to help children raise their learning levels, and computer training is available to all. Under Ms. Ferrell's leadership, Barry Farms has changed from a place devastated by violence and death to one of community and support.

Ms. Ferrell reported that, during the last several years, some young people from Barry Farm have been accepted at college. Many have obtained jobs as a consequence of training and mentoring that received from the programs that she helped bring to the development. She said,

> When the kids come out of school with a good grade point average and have a job waiting for them or go to college, it makes me so happy. Sometimes they were giving me kisses and things and said if it weren't for me being here they wouldn't have made it. I cried a lot.

Community Preservation and Development Corporation (CPDC)

In addition to the work of individuals, some organizations that are committed to the revitalization of extremely impoverished areas have done some amazing work.

CPDC was founded in 1989 by Eugene F. Ford, a developer in Washington, DC. CPDC was organized to create and preserve affordable housing. It gives major emphasis to helping residents strengthen their relationships with each other and with institutions that serve the community.

Edgewood Terrace is an apartment complex of 884 dwellings located near Catholic University in Northeast Washington. In 1995, twenty-two percent of residents lived below the poverty level, forty-five percent of the households received welfare, and forty-one percent had not graduated from high school. In the census tract where the development is located, eighty percent of the children under the age of eighteen were in single-parent households. Violent crimes in the area were thirty-eight per thousand; the figure for the city was twenty-five per thousand.[1] The Edgewood development, with its high crime rate and extensive social ills, was a challenge that CPDC undertook with the certainty that problems of this neighborhood could be overcome with the joint and committed efforts of the residents, the local and federal government, and local institutions and businesses.

The CPDC plan for Edgewood included community service programs with comprehensive and coordinated objectives. The goals were to (1) assist in the development of community leadership and to promote community interaction; (2) help residents identify their own strengths and talents and to use them to improve their own lives and life in the neighborhood; (3) help parents and children work together regularly and successfully to strengthen family bonds that are essential to the stabilization of community ties; (4) help residents increase cultural and educational experiences for themselves and their neighbors; (5) help residents strengthen their understanding of economic opportunities and initiate efforts to join the economic mainstream; (6) support residents in recognizing and thanking outstanding contributions of individual residents, thus encouraging others to increase their individual efforts and enhance the growing sense of pride in the community; (7) help residents strengthen their own capabilities to take full advantage of opportunities afforded by the mainstream economic system; and (8) help residents establish stronger and more extensive relationships with neighborhood institutions, including Catholic University.

CPDC's efforts to help residents began in 1991. As rehabilitation of the development began, residents were included in the discussion of plans for their homes. Eventually, most of the residents joined a resident council, which served to insure that their views were incorporated into policies and procedures. CPDC reports that enthusiasm for improvements increased the attendance at regular meetings from an average of ten to more than a hundred.

To enhance the growth of community among residents, CPDC inaugurated a requirement that all residents participate or volunteer in a community program activity. The programs, which residents and CPDC created, included homework assistance, after-school tutoring, coaching youth athletics, computer learning programs, youth mentoring, and assisting elderly residents with shopping.

CPDC's well known and highly acclaimed job-training center located at Edgewood Terrace is intended to assist residents and neighbors to achieve skills needed in the modern work force. This program, which began with a $1.2 million grant from the HUD and software from Microsoft Corporation has been enthusiastically received, not only by residents, but also by neighboring communities and national groups.

The computer learning center comprises more than sixty work stations equipped with office software, productivity applications, educational resources, reference materials, and more. Classes for beginning and intermediate skills are offered in Microsoft products (Word, Excel, PowerPoint and Access). These classes all use

Microsoft-approved curricula. Upon satisfactory completion of the series of courses for a particular application, a student is prepared to take the Microsoft Proficiency Certification Test. Upon passing the tests, students become Certified Microsoft Office Users.

Seventy percent of the students at the training center are on welfare and most are single mothers. Patricia Fisher, a young single mother, was earning minimum wage at a coffee shop when she began her training. After three months of training at the Center, she was employed at a policy research firm in a Washington suburb at twice the salary she received at the coffee shop. More than one hundred and eighty low-income residents of Washington, DC, have received training at the Center and are employed in jobs that make use of the computer training and pay living wages. The Edgewood community also has plans to install computers in each of the apartments in the development to make it one of the City's first "wired" communities.

The Edgewood program has been strongly endorsed by HUD, and the program has attracted both local and national attention for its success in establishing an environment where residents could envision a better life for themselves because of their improved ability to compete for jobs and care for their families. CPDC staff members are frequently asked to help other communities establish similar programs.

Though CPDC recognized that some residents required more support than others to make the leap from dependency to independent living, the program made it clear that it was the residents who had to succeed by reason of their commitment and concentration. This was made possible by CPDC's early recognition and use of promising candidates as models for others to emulate. The public ceremonies acknowledging the achievement of resident participants provided a path for resident pride in their community, their neighbors, and themselves. These experiences appear to have been the basis for a new and healthy community feeling among the residents of this once neglected housing development.

CPDC has established a record for creating affordable housing and establishing community services designed to enhance the social and economic well-being of at-risk families. CPDC President Leslie Steen said,

> When we approach a project like Edgewood Terrace, the rehabilitation of bricks and mortar is the first, critical step. However, it is the investment in community and the successful partnering with residents and businesses that will make the ultimate difference.

The Center for Mental Health

The Center for Mental Health, a well-established mental health service group, started a family-centered addiction recovery program with facilities in the Anacostia/Congress Heights area. Initiated and operated by Dr. Johanna Ferman, the program is centered on family participation in the recovery of patients. Its success has been widely acknowledged. The Center for Mental Health has conducted a Family Health Program in Anacostia since 1991. Its goals are to reduce the severity of impairment among children born to substance-abusing women, decrease the evidence and prevalence of drug and alcohol use among pregnant and postpartum women, encourage a drug-free life style, and strengthen families through intervention and support services. The Center employs an interdisciplinary team of skilled professionals that works closely with social service agencies in the area.

A major focus of the Center is its comprehensive therapeutic after-school program for children who are trying to cope with poverty, broken families, drugs, sexual abuse, and violence. The program is in session from 7:00 A.M. to 7:00 P.M., Monday through Friday. The sessions include emphasis on academic achievement.

The Center's services, which are integrated with family and community resources, reduces hospitalizations, residential and institutional care, child abuse, school drop outs, and the use of illegal drugs and alcohol. The efforts result in fewer children taking special education or remedial classes and helps parents pass high school equivalency tests, obtain jobs, and come off of welfare. Families and community are engaged as critically important resources for the ultimate improvement of the health of the Center's patients.

Hope VI

Without question, the most ambitious program to eliminate the problems associated with the clustering of large numbers of our poorest families in public housing was authorized by legislation enacted by the US Congress in 1992. The program, called Hope VI, provided grants and unprecedented flexibility to address the housing and social service needs of the residents. The legislation responded to recommendations by the National Commission on Severely Distressed Public Housing. The Commission recommended a combination of physical, managerial and social improvements to relieve public housing distress. Hope VI was intended to provide benefits to public housing residents and the residents of communities adjacent to the improved sites.

During his tenure as Secretary of HUD, Henry Cisneros placed high priority on the potential of Hope VI not only to alleviate the wretched conditions under which the poorest of the poor lived in public housing, but also to revitalize American cities. Municipal services were in disarray and many cities lost significant populations as the result of concentrated poverty. Operating costs were up and revenues were down. Urban living was at a point of lowest appeal.

Housing Authority leaders from large cities across the nation saw Hope VI as a program that would help to eliminate the problems of their housing. The official objectives of Hope VI do not specify the elimination of the isolation of the poorest of the poor families and the tragic consequences that have accompanied it. However, Hope VI was seen as a way to reinvent housing for the poor by carefully blending it with housing for the nonpoor and to ensure that the design is attractive and supports the creation and maintenance of communities and strong families.

The first Hope VI project in Washington, DC, was the Ellen Wilson Public Housing Development located on Capitol Hill, less than ten blocks from the US Capitol building. This project was built for poor white families. Over the next decade it, like many other public housing developments in the city, lost tenants as budgets for regular maintenance and repairs diminished. Eventually it was totally vacant and remained so for sometime. I was a member of a small group of interested citizens who met to discuss the potential for the desolate development. There was unanimous consent that the development needed to be dismantled and replaced with housing that was more in keeping with the design of most housing in the Capitol Hill District.

With resources provided under the Hope VI program, the Ellen Wilson development was demolished and rebuilt as a housing development for middle income and moderate income renters and homeowners. It stands as proud testimony to good judgment of the sponsors of Hope VI who were confident that a well-balanced development for the poor and nonpoor would produce a stable and peaceful community. Not only did the development market well, but it also had a stabilizing influence on the privately owned, single-family housing that surrounds it.

Hope VI also was the program that permitted the city to demolish the Valley Green Public Housing Project in the Far Southeast that is known far and wide for its crime and disorder. With the full commitment of Jackie Massey and her small group of courageous neighbors, the Hope VI program was embraced and Valley Green is now a beautiful development of single-family homes mixed with garden apartments serving both the poor and nonpoor who own or rent their new homes.

Several other local public housing projects in the nation's capital are either active Hope VI projects or are planned to become so.

Housing Authorities have responded to the Hope VI program in every section of the country. Chicago, Illinois submitted a plan to HUD to transform its public housing by demolishing dilapidated skyscrapers and replacing them with low-rise structures to accommodate mixed income tenants.[2] This is a five-year program at a cost of $1.5 billion. The plan is well underway to replace sixteen thousand existing apartments with more than twenty-four thousand new or rehabilitated dwellings.

Baltimore was among the first large housing authorities to undertake major Hope VI efforts. Lexington Terrace and Lafayette Courts, which were built in the 1950s, included both high-rise and garden-type apartment buildings. Over the years the small funds for operation and increased vandalism resulted in extensive deterioration. Drug activity increased to momentous levels. Many families were compelled to leave and few were attracted to come. The housing authority concluded that the high rises conceptually were the wrong idea. Residents felt stigmatized to be living in high-rise buildings, which were the scenes of so much disorder and despair. They wanted to live in town houses "like everybody else does."

The Housing Authority's experiences with high-rise developments for families led them to conclude that high rises were not the ideal configuration for dwellings to serve poor families. Many residents had expressed the desire to live in row houses.

Row houses for rent and for sale to accommodate the poor and the nonpoor were designed to replace deteriorated high rises. The results have been highly praised. Social and economic conditions have improved and the Housing Authority of Baltimore City has retained its reputation for outstanding service.

Baltimore's aggressive Hope VI program has produced some opposition, however. The "resettlement" of low-income residents in middle-class neighborhoods has some people upset.[3] For some residents and human service advocates, the greatest fear is that the so-called balanced communities mean fewer dwellings for the poor.

The Philadelphia Housing Authority, which received more than $100 million in Hope VI revitalization funds in 1993, embraced the Hope VI program as the opportunity "to transform entire neighborhoods, uplifting communities and, most importantly, improving the quality of life of our residents and our neighbors."[4]

The enthusiastic use of the Hope VI program by a wide cross-section of local housing authorities is clear evidence that the public housing officials were seeking an acceptable means of restoring an image of competence and vision.

Hope VI provided a way to improve housing quality and livability and also a way to attract stable families. Whether stated or not, most of the plans for the use of Hope VI would result in the creation of neighborhoods where families with a range of incomes and life experiences would become neighbors. The more balanced range of income should provide leaven to help the poor families find ways to attain a new level of independence and a respectable status among their neighbors.

The funding for HOPE VI has been discontinued by Congress at the request of President George W. Bush. This will make it difficult to grow healthy social environments for the poor. It is clear, however, that the time is not for complacency. We must remember that the public housing program began with a clear call to help poor families achieve a state of independent living. We must bring back that goal.

Notes

1. James Zabora Dean, *Edgewood Terrace Needs Assesment* (Washington, DC: Catholic University of America School of Social Work, March 23, 1994), 24–26.
2. Robert Novak, ""HUD v. Chicago," *The Washington Post,* 4 November 1999, A24.
3. Otto, Mary, "Public Housing Strategy Riles Baltimore Neighbors: Some Residents Resist Plan to Scatter Poor Throughout Neighborhood," *The Washington Post*, 9 November 2000, A11.
4. The Philadelphia Housing Authority, *HOPE VI: Richard Allen Homes, Martin Luther King Plaza, Schuylkill Falls* (Philadelphia: The Philadelphia Housing Authority, n.d.), 1–4.

Chapter 12

Conclusions and Recommendations

In the past, adequate housing was provided for the poor to improve their health and, more important, to change their overwhelmingly immoral ways. In spite of years of experience in England and the United States that failed to validate the correlation between poor housing and immorality, there have been few who have questioned the basic thesis. Even today advocates of housing for the poor seem unmindful of the history of social disorder that has developed as the poor have been isolated in significant numbers. Their advocacy of improved housing for the poor continues to be based on the vague assumption that, somehow or other, better housing will improve social and economic conditions.

Though it did not benefit the poor socially, there is little question that physically improved housing dramatically improved the health of the poor. Prior to public housing, the slums in America's largest cities had allowed very serious health problems to proliferate. The impact of improved housing upon physical health, however, did not solve all of the problems of the poor.

The dismal networking system in impoverished communities exacerbates the already limited job opportunities. For many people, networking is the means by which they obtain information about employment opportunities. Friends and relatives often make excellent job resources. In impoverished communities, however, the lines of communication between neighbors are poor. Further, their connection with the main world of business is limited. Thus, information about opportunities is limited.

Theories about the deterioration faced by those living in impoverished urban areas have instead focused on issues other than their concentration. Some observers have concluded that the urban poor are not naturally endowed with the aptitude to participate fully in society. If they possess the inherent ability to succeed, say these observers, then the poor will rise on their own.

Other students of urban issues have concluded that people living in concentrated poverty cannot function on their own and require extensive professional aid. Such aid, provided by both public and private agencies whose sole mission is to help the poor, is the only remedy for the problems associated with concentrated poverty. Only the experience and knowledge of trained professionals can begin to rectify the myriad problems associated with severely impoverished areas.

A third group of observers feels strongly that low income is the sole cause of deteriorated areas and that the promotion of a robust economy can help to turn the tide of such depravity. Increased investments in small business and local infrastructure in poor communities can help families become independent. The development of a strong economy is the means by which to achieve stable neighborhoods.

Missing from these arguments is the very real impact of isolated poverty. That the poor are often clustered together and segregated from the rest of society seems to be an obvious and inevitable fact of life. There is very little understanding among urban observers that social isolation has been the basis for much of the crime and social disorder.

There have been numerous well-intentioned programs, in addition to public housing, that have been created throughout the years to battle poverty. Indeed, most programs for the poor come from noble beginnings. However, these programs have not always produced positive consequences.

It is time that we realize the importance of our previous mistakes and move toward a comprehensive plan to alleviate the pain and misery associated with urban poverty. We as a nation can no longer champion equality when so many of our citizens are systematically denied opportunities. We must move forward with an aggressive plan.

In the previous chapter, we described several efforts that we feel are exemplary. However, these programs alone will not solve all of the problems of the urban poor. They are only a beginning, a glimpse of what can be accomplished when people are provided the opportunity to change their lives.

Indeed, there is no easy solution or magic formula that will erase the deep-seated problems found in many cities. Patience will be critical if we are to be serious in undertaking social change. Our recurring impatience has done little service in situations that require extreme attention, such as those in impoverished, urban areas.

We must open our minds to new ideas that can change our cities. We must build consensus about those ideas by urging the contribution of resources from varying sectors of our society, from business and philanthropic organizations to government and community members. Years of experience with mistaken strategies should teach us something about what must actually be done, but even before we can create actual strategies to improve the lives of the poor, we must set out a general ethos to guide those strategies.

Human growth, stability, and development are primarily dependent upon a social and economic environment that encourages, supports, and affirms the right, duty, and ability of its members to be all that they can be. That environment is not present where we have isolated large numbers of our poorest and most troubled citizens. We are convinced that our future depends upon our recognition of the compelling role of community and family as basic factors in stabilizing and invigorating our democracy.

All healthy communities require the leaven of those who have their feet firmly on the ladder to independent living and who will help their neighbors join them. Though most often taken for granted where it exists, where leaven is absent, the neighborhood remains without stability.

Intent

There is little question that early efforts to provide subsidized housing were intended to assist families that were seeking a better life.

The intention of the Housing Act of 1937, which authorized the national low-rent public housing program, was to "promote the general welfare of the Nation." It was expected that the new housing opportunities would eliminate the root causes of much of the nation's crime, social distress and attendant costs.

Families aided in the early days of public housing proved to be a representative cross-section of the nation's low-income population. They were typically two-parent families with employment as the primary source of income. Careful examination of credit and social histories served to assure their selection as tenants. Stability and order was typical in public housing developments in the early years of the program.

As the years passed and more and more of the poorest families were rehoused in decent, safe, and sanitary housing in many large cities, the environment became increasingly indecent, unsafe, and unstable.

There were some warnings that the gradual change in public housing toward a preponderance of the poorest and most troubled families was unhealthy.[1] Among proponents of priority consideration of the poorest of the poor in public housing, there was the conviction that serving the most needy first was both just and moral. Indeed, in many quarters it would have been political suicide to suggest that providing housing exclusively for our poorest citizens would bring unprecedented disorder.

Consequence:
Deterioration of Community and Family Life

As the poorest of the poor became the predominant beneficiaries of public housing, more stable residents moved out. Some applicants who were more stable simply refused offers of public housing when they became aware of intense problems in some housing developments. Only the most desperate applicants accepted offers of vacant units, and they were predominantly single-parent families on public assistance.

Often single parents in public housing are young and female. They are sometimes unprepared for the demanding responsibility of raising children and managing a household because they themselves have not received the nurturing that leads to maturity. These young people are faced with severe financial, emotional, and physical problems. Lacking the confidence to meet the problems alone, they are further frustrated when all about them, their neighbors face the same dilemma.

Many single mothers who reside in public housing are involved in some form of an ongoing sexual relationship. Often, short-term boyfriends who come to visit young mothers are disruptive. Some children resent the visitors. Physical and verbal abuse from both sides can result. Many teenage males leave home. Young females are sometimes the object of the advances of their mother's suitor, which creates even more inflammatory problems. Great frustration arises as these problems become more widespread and irritability becomes commonplace.

Many single parents living in public and subsidized housing are without the support of extended family and friends. Some are members of deeply fractured families in which communication is infrequent.

Further, friendships among the isolated poor are impeded by ever-present emergencies. Residents who are absorbed by a myriad of grievous problems are oftentimes unable to give thought and time to forming community or to offer their children the nurturing required for healthy growth and maturation.

Consequence:
Deterioration of Public Education

Learning occurs in the home and in schools. It is the ability and willingness to learn, which we hope will be encouraged outside of school, that students should bring to the classroom. The teacher's role in the learning process is to provide a structured program to give order to the learning experience. Students are at a great advantage if their parents encourage their curiosity and provide clear answers to their questions. Many poor, single parents, who are confronted by daily emergencies, respond to questions from inquisitive children with "Don't bother me" or "Go look at television," or even worse, a slap. Where that kind of response is prevalent, the natural propensity toward inquisitiveness may be blunted. Parents who are increasingly burdened with other problems often do not discuss school with their children or become involved in Parent-Teacher Associations. Without parental and community nurturing, children are handicapped when they enter school.

Teachers who work in schools that serve the poorest of the poor are confronted by students who are unprepared with basic knowledge and diminished curiosity. When many students experience significant problems at home, and bring them into the classroom, schools find themselves ill equipped to handle increasing disruptions.

The improvement of education depends upon the reestablishment of family and community in the traditional roles of preparing and supporting their children in the learning process. The impact on children of the hours that they spend outside the formal classroom situation is decisive in the learning process. Helping to make those hours outside of school productive is a challenge that must be met by families, schools, and communities together.

In communities with successful schools, particularly successful public schools, the role of parents is of tremendous importance. Though it is widely understood that in the poorest communities, the level of learning is low for many students from poor families and that the level of parental participation in the formal education of their children is low, the problems with urban education are most often deemed simply a failure of schools.

Consequence:
Deterioration of Social Services

Most human service agencies have been overwhelmed by the intensity and magnitude of the problems of the isolated poor. There have been many gallant efforts to remedy the problems, but the level of distress has been unyielding. It appeared that the more services were rendered, the worse the problems became. As severely impoverished areas became more distressed, service agencies and advocates of the poor became more desperate both to meet the growing need and to retain their reputations for effective service.

Many service agencies were required to increase the sizes of their caseloads as problems grew because of the concentration of poverty. Relationships between workers and clients sometimes were frayed. Nevertheless, the increasingly influential role of human service agencies in isolated neighborhoods established these institutions as community leaders. The role of the few residents who might have dared to voice the concerns of the neighborhood was diminished.

Before the concentration of the poor raised the level of distress, the social service-client relationship was substantially different. Employees of social service agencies frequently visited the homes of their clients. The visits were important to the communication process. The person-to-person meetings permitted communication of feelings and allowed for observations critical to understanding the true status of besieged clients. As those relationships became less personal, the services became less effective.

As a source of reliable help for immigrants and migrants who were seeking to reestablish themselves, social service agencies were among the first to be called to help the isolated poor. In previous decades, settlement houses had served as neighborhood centers where newcomers sought assistance and where activities for all ages served to germinate the seeds of community.

Some human service agencies plan for the future as though the problems they seek to alleviate will always be present. As more funds are available to support efforts to help the poor, more agencies are constructing or buying permanent buildings to accommodate their programs. For the visitor, an area lined with buildings occupied by services to the poor is a "poor neighborhood." Even if the nearby poor ultimately become nonpoor, the buildings remain centers of active service and the characterization of "poor neighborhood" remains unchanged. Permanent office buildings are testimony to the confidence of the service agency that the need for their services is perpetual or, to put it negatively, the services are not intended to eliminate the problem.

Consequence:
Crime

There is little question that the slums have produced many children who are starved for affection because their mothers were crushed with emergencies, unhappy with themselves, and hopeless about the future. There is also little question that children raised without affection are often those who strike out against humanity and become delinquents. The more the unloved strike out, the more often and more severely they are punished until at last they die by the hand of violence or are confined to one of our prisons.

Rarely has there been public discussion of the possibility that the public, through its government and under continuous pressure from advocates in the public and private sector, has produced social environments that beget crime, death, and despair. It is our conclusion that the social environment in many large clusters of publicly subsidized housing generated crime and other social disorder at unprecedented levels in our society.

Consequence:
Deterioration of Neighborhood Businesses

Not only are the isolated poor afflicted by despair, but they find it more difficult to purchase goods and services of standard quality at reasonable prices. Businesses in isolated areas of impoverishment are more frequently the victims of robbery and violence. Eventually the cost to isolated areas of impoverishment came to include losses in business revenue, sales taxes to the community, and part-time employment opportunities for young people.

The impact of the absence of viable businesses is yet another reason for the more stable families to find other places to live. Unlike the poorer neighborhoods during the early decades of the twentieth century, resident ownership of small shops that serve neighbors is now seldom found. Stable communities of lower-income families in the "old days" included businesses that were owned or at least operated by local residents.

Recommendations

It has become undeniably apparent that the detachment between "mainstream" society and the urban poor has been truly devastating. There is no question that there is a pervasive sentiment among the poor that they are outcasts. Many impoverished residents are convinced that their mistreatment is calculated. It is not difficult to understand why so many urban, impoverished African Americans feel excluded from the majority of society. The image portrayed of them in the media is incessantly that of violent, irresponsible people. They are without the benefit of strong families and community.

The ideal solution to the concentration of poverty would be to have all new housing developments, apartments, and single-family homes include some small number for impoverished people no matter where they are, regardless of whether they are funded by government or privately sponsored. This is a difficult and very controversial issue, but we should not let ourselves be deterred from meeting the challenge.

Eliminating the isolation of the poor would lead to several important changes. As the poor experience an increased sense of self-worth and mainstream involvement, they will begin to take steps to protect and retain their new status. We can expect a decrease in crime and health problems and a gradual improvement in the quality of life. All of this will ultimately contribute to the fiscal and social stability of cities. Families and communities would again become reliable foundations for our civility and stability. The challenge we face is to show conclusively the connection between the isolated poor and the many costs to the country. These costs are not only in terms of dollars, but also include the cost in terms of lives and strengths and the contribution of its citizenry that is lost because we concentrate the poor.

Many advocates for the poor and concerned members of society may wonder whether the suggestion that the poor be incorporated into mainstream society suggests the elimination or dilution of programs that aid the poor. It is not the obliteration of programs that offer positive, supportive aid that we recommend. Those programs must recognize that family and community restoration are cardinal elements of successful assistance to human growth and development.

We should create a national commission to monitor the status of programs that are aimed at moving the poor toward self-sufficiency.

Such a commission should have the responsibility to endorse programs, establish time schedules, and develop strategies to guide the change from poverty to independence. States and cities should establish similar commissions to coordinate efforts and transfer useful information across the country. The time has come for us all to accept the basic conclusion that, in spite of our best efforts, the isolation of impoverished families from the daily cycle of economic, social, and cultural activities of the society of which they are a part leads inevitably to more all-consuming poverty and despair. The impoverished become the victims of the very efforts that seek their redemption. The price of this outcome should be unacceptable to all.

The HOPE VI program was the beginning of such an endeavor. There were, however, few efforts in the media to explain the objectives of HOPE VI. We did not see it in newspaper stories or on television. Most people did not know what it was intended to do, and even when the major newspapers wrote stories about HOPE VI, they did not explain the program in detail.

The main purpose of the program is to eliminate problems that are manifested because some people are quarantined. This is not a new conviction about this issue. It's been going on for many years, but we have never embraced it in public policy, except with HOPE VI. Even this program was not as effective as it could have been because the story behind isolated poverty was not told.

Remaining Committed to Growing Community

Community is essentially a social immune system. The social immune system enforces the principle of belonging. In the course of life in a community, children, with the guidance of parents and neighbors, come to understand that they belong to a stable group. Those who share community come to accept behavioral requirements that must be honored if one is to maintain membership. Members in good standing can expect neighbors to come to their rescue in times of trouble. They can expect to be complimented and held in higher regard when they excel. Individuals are proud to be members and constantly seek to preserve the respect and support of their neighbors. Communities emerge naturally as families facing common challenges and opportunities instinctively solicit each other for support. Where the poorest of the poor are isolated, the evolution of community is thwarted both by the controls held by landlords and ever-present human service organizations. Poor residents who are potential leaders are often reluctant to be aggressive in organizing the strength of their neighbors. Too often they have been identified as "trouble makers."

Nonetheless, the vision of community and its life-saving support for poor residents must be encouraged even as we seek ways to reduce their isolation.

A few neighbors resist community, finding anonymity an advantage; others have strong relationships elsewhere that command their continued allegiance and commitment. Community does not require all of its members to be close friends. It requires neighbors to respect each other and honor the shared responsibilities for the common good. Even if they are now and again tempted to participate in unconventional activities, community relationships will generally tend to dissuade such action. Without community, the poor, particularly the clustered poor, have little immunity to the deceptive offers of a quick fix. Absent a social immune system, the poor come to be counted as the most immoral, the most criminal, and the most dishonest of all members of society.

As with the immune system of the human body, the community-based immune system is at work all day, every day. Members of a community react to protect community interests. The social immune systems protect community members from participation in behavior that is destructive to themselves and to others.

The immune system in isolated neighborhoods of the poorest of the poor is absent because of a combination of undeveloped leadership; domineering services effectively inhibit its emergence. Luc De Schepper wrote in *Full of Life: How to Achieve and Maintain Peak Immunity*,

> The immune system is an example of perfect democracy in which each member performs its task without being controlled by a central organ. It provides a twenty-four hour security system always on the alert for viruses, harmful bacteria, fungi, protozoa . . . even malignant cells.[2]

The term "community-building," however, is not a valid characterization of the process that leads to the creation of community. "Building" is associated with assembling or erecting or framing or producing. The experience in the Anacostia/Congress Heights area leads to the conclusion that community must be grown. It is an act that must be nurtured. The community is like a plant that requires proper soil, water, and light. A plant withers away when not provided with proper care. A community is not something that an outsider can construct. The best the outsider can do is to fertilize the seed.

The Learning Environment

We must nurture students and counsel parents in effective ways to support their children's learning. That approach has been used successfully in some communities in Washington, DC. Without question, officials and teachers of children in isolated communities must come to understand the source of the problem that has confounded them.

It is essential to develop new and aggressive strategies to engage parents in efforts to help their children learn. The learning process must be a continuous, everyday process that engages the whole community in constantly increasing opportunities for children to learn.

As families and communities join in the creation of a learning environment for their children, they too will become more stable and confident of the future. The objective of a learning environment must be to encourage the normal curiosity of all children and adults. This is not to suggest that a learning environment will replace public schools. It is essential that public school officials help to design and monitor the learning environment.

However, the learning environment must also be the product of the community and its constituent families. The learning environment created by families and communities must focus on reading, visits to cultural centers, and encouraging children to keep diaries of their experiences.

Because many children in the Anacostia/Congress Heights neighborhood were not the beneficiaries of sustained nurturing, we are in the process growing a Neighborhood Learning Environment. Modeled after a program at the Barry Farm Public Housing Project and the Birney Elementary School, the program has four critical components. The first component is reading clubs for children from six to sixteen years of age. The clubs will be initiated in all child care centers, churches, and libraries in the neighborhood. Parents of all children are required to give a few hours to supervise clubs, serve snacks, and participate as chaperones on field trips. The content of the reading will be recommended by the schools and local libraries to assure its relevance to the school curriculum. The second component is to begin a program of field trips to offer children an opportunity to see many of the subjects about which they read. Third, gradually the children will be encouraged to take notes about their reading and their visits. Those notes will be carefully preserved in notebooks and will serve as references when they present their parents, teachers, and friends with evidence of their learning. Fourth, there will be evaluations of the program by educators and parents.

It is important that our program keep the community informed and reward outstanding readers, tutors, and volunteers who will be basic to the learning environment. Annual celebrations of achievements and announcements of plans for the next year should be considered. Close coordination with schools must be a commitment.

The purpose of this program is to rekindle the curiosity and confidence that the children must have to progress from one grade to another and to understand the world around them. This program is a supplement to reinvigorate the natural curiosity of children living in Anacostia. We are confident that the impact of this program on the children will drastically improve their school performances and gradually help them to be a significant influence on their urban neighborhoods. However, the program has not yet been funded.

Recognition of Family and Community

The most critical failure of the human service organizations has been their unwillingness to recognize the indispensable role of families and community in the amelioration of the problems that are endured by isolated families. It is important to repeat that, in isolation, few residents have resourceful families or a stable community to assist them in their daily efforts to survive. The process of human service should include an assessment of the conditions of families and community. Where those conditions are weak, human service agencies should support efforts to strengthen them so as to assure the support of the community for the successful outcome of services rendered. This is a heavy burden to impose on any one agency. Because most families are known to several human service agencies simultaneously, it is important that the agencies unite in efforts to strengthen families and community. Stronger support from families and community will enhance the value of agency services.

The coordination of human services that are provided by both government and private charities is an essential function if their efforts are to have a salutary effect. This is especially true in neighborhoods where social problems are most intense.

Early in our urban experience, settlement houses earned the respect of the families that they served and were treasured by the communities where they were located. By the time the new problem of the clustered poor became evident, settlement houses were no longer a major part of the social service structure. Settlement houses came into being primarily with migration from Europe. These institutions were intended to help the migrants adjust themselves to a new country in every way, from language and music to recreation. It was a family-centered program.

The settlement house's work was primarily to help the community come together, to do things together. It was a part of the community structure. There was no need to have caseworkers handle every family issue. Particular family issues might have arisen, but they were handled by the community rather than by professional workers in the settlement houses.

Social work, like many other professions, has become more highly specialized. As it became more highly specialized and moved into communities and worked with families with different issues, the role of the settlement house diminished.

One advantage that the settlement houses had over social work as we now know it is that they generally were open every day of the week and they were open until late at night. They did not have office hours. It was a neighborhood institution. It was there constantly, and people who had trouble could go in and talk to the settlement house director and get some advice. This is not to say that a return to settlement houses is the ideal solution, but the model that they embody, that of a community entity, is a strong model for our human service organizations today.

There is no human service that is not inherently dependent upon the underpinning of community and family to achieve a dependable effectiveness. The successful treatment of social disorder requires a stable community setting. In the absence of that setting, even the most consummate professional service is unlikely to achieve a significant reduction in the intensity or scope of the problem. With the sensitive recruitment of a community's resources, institutions, and leaders, the chances for meaningful improvement can be remarkable. It is therefore essential that human service programs that help families in isolated developments include in their plans the cultivation of community resources, institutions, and individuals to share in all efforts to help stabilize families and bring order to neighborhoods. The community resources will assure that human service efforts are at work twenty-four hours a day, seven days a week. Thus, the effort becomes a community objective that will not only aid those neighbors who are the most deeply distressed, but also will help to establish an ongoing community commitment to respond to the needs of its members. Here we stress again the unique ability of strong communities to provide preventive and remedial help to their own. In the past, human service programs were intended to assist troubled families in overcoming problems that prevented stability and growth.

The Anacostia/Congress Heights Partnership found the following steps to be essential in encouraging the evolution of community:

1. Ask the residents what they envision as improvements needed in the neighborhoods and their families.

2. Solicit the participation of neighborhood churches, schools, and civic groups in support of residents' efforts to improve life where they live.

3. Support neighborhood-chosen leaders to organize their meetings to establish objectives and plans to achieve them.

4. Help leaders solicit outside assistance in achieving their objective.

5. Emphasize the need to establish regular community recognition of the achievements of its residents, including those of children.

6. Help the residents plan regular community celebrations of holidays with all residents assuming some responsibilities for success.

7. Help outside groups understand how important it is for residents to know they can make a difference in the quality of their own lives and that of the city.

There must come to be agreement among advocates, human service givers, and neighborhood leaders that *community* is the underlying force that supports human services. Human service leaders must come to acknowledge that theirs is a helping role, not a redeeming one.

In most neighborhoods, before government became involved in housing development, communities were present because residents found a need for each other in meeting common objectives. It was not until the large isolated areas of troubled impoverishment were built that the earlier assumption of citizen support and cooperation began to be unreliable.

The path to stable life in our cities requires us to understand that humans, like all living creatures, require nurturing to achieve maturity. Families and community have been the foundation for human survival. Unless and until we find a viable substitute, we must preserve both.

Our failure to recognize and respond to the subtle signs of human deterioration as we sought to meet the needs for affordable and decent housing must serve as a warning for our future. That experience must convince us that corroding conditions that are allowed to fester in certain parts of society ultimately bring grief to us all. In a world filled with ambitious people seeking to establish themselves and their interests, we must not neglect the basic human need for continuous affirmation that can only come from family and community. There is no freedom when one is nameless and unrecognized even in one's own neighborhood. Only with the quiet confirmation of another can life have meaning.

With our urban population projected to increase dramatically in this new millenium, the need for strong communities and families is more urgent than ever. The fate of generations to come depend largely on our success in restoring these basic components of civilized living.

Notes

1. Rainwater, Lee, *Behind Ghetto Walls: Black Families in a Federal Slum* (Chicago: Aldine Publishing Company, 1970), 1–7.
2. Luc De Schepper, *Full of Life: How to Achieve and Maintain Peak Immunity* (Los Angeles: Tale Weaver Publishing, 1991), 28–29.

Bibliography

Alley Dwelling Authority of the District of Columbia. *Slum Reclamation and Rehousing.* Washington, DC: Alley Dwelling Authority of Washington, DC, 1936.

Andrew, John A. *Lyndon Johnson and the Great Society.* Chicago: Ivan P. Dee, 1998.

Atkins, Gordon. *Health, Housing, and Poverty in New York City: 1865–1898.* Ph.D. diss., Columbia University, 1947.

Bailey, Anne Lowrey. "Jimmy Carter's War on Poverty." *The Chronicle of Philanthropy* (12 January 1993), 6–15.

Belkin, Lisa. *Show Me a Hero: A Tale of Murder, Race, Suicide, and Redemption.* Boston: Little Brown, 1999.

Best, Gardy Dean. *Pride, Prejudice, and Politics: Roosevelt and Recovery, 1933–1938.* New York: Praeger, 1991.

Borchert, James. *Alley Life in Washington.* Urbana: University of Illinois Press, 1980.

Bureau of Justice Statistics. "Criminal Offenders Statistics, Drug Control Budget, Homicide Trends in the United States." *Sourcebook of Criminal Justice Statistics.* Washington, DC: Bureau of Justice Statistics, 1999.

Burke, Paul. *A Picture of Subsidized Households in 1997: United States: Totals and Agencies with over 500 Units.* Washington, DC: Office of Policy Development and Research, Office of Economic Affairs, Division of Housing and Demographic Analysis; Department of Housing and Urban Development, 1997.

Caraley, Demetrios, Ed. *Critical Issues for Clinton's Domestic Agenda: Essays from Political Science Quarterly.* New York: The Academy of Political Science, 1994.

Center for Public Affairs, National League of Cities. *The National League of Cities Handbook: A Guide to Services and Participation.* Washington, DC: The National League of Cities, 1994.

Chideya, Farai, Michele Ingrassia, Vern E. Smith, and Pat Wingert. "Endangered Family: For Many African Americans, Marriage and Childbearing Do Not Go Together." *Newsweek* (August 30, 1993): 16–27.

City of East Cleveland, and Arthur D. Little, Inc. *Response to Urban Change.* Cleveland, Ohio: City of Cleveland, 1969.

Cityscape: A Journal of Policy Development and Research Commemorating the 30th Anniversary of the Fair Housing Act 4, no. 3., 1999.

Conkin, Paul K. *The New Deal.* Wheeling, Illinois: Harlan Davidson, Inc., 1967.

Corlibaly, Modibo, Rodney D. Green, and David M. Jones. *Segregation in Federally Subsidized Low-Income Housing in the United States*. Westport, Connecticut: Praeger, 1998.

DeForest, Robert W., and Lawrence Veiller. *The Tenement House Problem; Including the Report of the New York State Tenement House Commission of 1900* (Vol. 1). New York: MacMillan Co., 1903.

DeLeeuw, Frank. *Operating Costs in Public Housing*. Washington, DC: Urban Institute, 1969.

Department of Housing and Urban Development, Housing Assistance Administration, Statistics Branch. *Families Moving into Low-Rent Housing: Calendar Year 1967*. Washington, DC: Government Printing Office, 1969.

Department of Housing and Urban Development, Housing Assistance Administration, Statistics Branch. *Families Moving Into Low-Rent Housing: January 1–September 30, 1968*. Washington, DC: Government Printing Office, 1969.

————. *Families in Low Rent Projects: Families Reexamined During Year*. Washington, DC: Government Printing Office, 1968.

————. *Families in Low-Rent Projects: Families Reexamined for Continued Occupancy Twelve Months Ending September 30, 1970*. Washington, DC: Government Printing Office, 1971.

————. *Families in Low-Rent Projects: Families Reexamined During Calendar Year 1967 for Continued Occupancy*. Washington, DC: Government Printing Office, 1969.

Department of Housing and Urban Development. Office of Housing Management, Statistics Branch. *Families in Low-Rent Projects: Families Reexamined for Continued Occupancy Twelve Months Ending September 30, 1969*. Washington, DC: Government Printing Office, 1971.

————. *Families Moving Into Low-Rent Housing: October 1, 1969–September 30, 1970*. Washington, DC: Government Printing Office, 1971

Fannie Mae. *Housing Policies for Distressed Urban Neighborhoods. Housing Policy Debate, 4*, no. 3 (1993). 253–490.

Fishman, W. J. *East End 1888: Life in a London Borough Among the Laboring Poor*. Philadelphia: Temple University Press, 1988.

Gardner, John W. *Building Community*. New York: The Free Press, 1991.

Goldman, Martin S. *Makers of America, John F. Kennedy: Portrait of a President*. New York: Facts on File, Inc., 1995.

Haar, Charles. *Between the Idea and the Reality: A Study in the Origin, Fate, and Legacy of the Model Cities Program*. Toronto: Little Brown, 1975.

Hays, R. Allen. *The Federal Government and Urban Housing*. Albany, New York: SUNY Press, 1985.

Hearings Before the Committee on Banking and Currency, H.R. 4009. 81st Congress, 1st Sess., 1950.

Housing Authority, Baltimore City. *Annual Report*. Baltimore, MD: Housing Authority, Baltimore City, 1995.

Housing Authority, City of Newark. *Progress Report: 1997–1998*. Newark, New Jersey: Housing Authority, City of Newark, 1999.

Huthmacher, J. Joseph. *Senator Robert F. Wagner and the Rise of Urban Liberalism*. New York: Atheneum, 1968.

Jencks, Christopher, and Paul E. Peterson, Eds. *The Urban Underclass*. Washington, DC: The Brookings Institution, 1991.

Koeber, George M. *The History and Development of the Housing Movement in the City of Washington, DC*. Washington, DC: Washington Sanitary Housing Companies, 1925.

Kretzmann, John P., and John L. McKnight. *Building Communities from the Inside Out: A Path Toward finding and Mobilizing a Community's Assets*. Chicago: Center for Urban Affairs and Policy Research, Neighborhood Innovations Network, Northwestern University, ACTA Publications, 1993.

Lynn, Laurence E., and Michael McGeary, Eds. *Inner City Poverty in the United States*. Washington, DC: Committee on National Urban Policy, National Research Council. National Academy Press, 1990.

Mason, Joseph. *History of Housing in the US, 1930–1980*. Houston, Texas: Gulf Publishing Co., 1982.

Matusow, Allen J. *Nixon's Economy: Booms, Busts, Dollars, and Votes*. Lawrence: University Press of Kansas, 1998.

McKnight, John. *The Careless Society: Community and its Counterfeits*. New York: Basic Books, 1995.

Moynihan, Daniel Patrick. *Maximum Feasible Misunderstanding: Community Action in the War on Poverty*. New York: The Free Press, 1969.

Murray, Margaret S. "Low-Income Renter Housing: Another View of the Tough Choice." *Journal of Housing Research*, 8, no. 1 (1997), 27–52.

Nathan Associates, Inc. *The Likely Impacts of Rent De-control on District of Columbia Residents*. Submitted to District of Columbia Financial Responsibility and Management Assistance Authority, 19 June 2000.

National Capital Housing Authority. *Annual Report*. Washington, DC: Government Printing Office, 1945.

———. *Large Family-rent Subsidy Demonstration Project*. Washington, DC: NCHA, 1966.

National Research Council. *Inner City Poverty in the United States*. Washington, DC: National Academy Press, 1990.

Nenno, Mary K. *Ending the Stalemate: Moving Housing and Urban Development into the Mainstream of America's Future*. New York: University Press of America, 1996.

Newark Redevelopment and Housing Authority. *Public Housing: Master Plan*. Newark, New Jersey: Newark Redevelopment and Housing Authority, 1984.

Ormond, Barbara A., and Randall R. Bovbjerg. *The Changing Hospital Sector in Washington, DC: Implications for the Poor*. Washington, DC: The Urban Institute, 1998.

Peattie, Lisa Redfield. "Public Housing: Urban Slums Under Public Management." *In Race, Change, and Urban Society*. Peter Orleans and William Russell Ellis, Jr., Eds. Beverly Hills, California: Sage Publications, 1971.

Philadelphia Housing Authority. *Annual Report*. Philadelphia, PA: Philadelphia Housing Authority, 1998.

Poverty Reference Bureau. *A New Look at Poverty*. Washington, DC: Government Printing Office, 1997.

Randolph, Norman, and Edsel Erickson. *Gangs, My Town, and the Nation*. Holmes Beach, Florida: Learning Publications, Inc., 1996.

Reiss, Albert J., and Michael Tonry, Eds. *Communities and Crime*. Chicago: The University of Chicago Press, 1986.

Riis, Jacob A. *A Ten Years" War: An Account of the Battle with the Slum in New York:* Books for Libraries Press, 1969.

Riis, Jacob. *The Battle with the Slums.* 1902. Reprint, Montclair, New Jersey: Patterson Smith.

Sabol, William J. *Crime Control and Common Sense Assumptions Underlying the Expansion of the Prison Population*. Washington, DC: The Urban Institute, 1998.

Sabol, William J., and James P. Lynch. *Crime Policy Report: Did Getting Tough on Crime Pay?* Washington, DC: The Urban Institute, 997.

Sampson, Robert J., and Janet L. Laureitsen. *Violent Victimization and Offending..*

Sampson, Robert J., Stephen W. Raudenbush, and Felton Earls. "Neighborhoods and Violent Crime: A Multilevel Study of Collective Efficacy," *Science*, 1997, *18-24*.

Schorr, A. L. "How the Poor Are Housed." In *Urban Housing*, W. L. C. Wheaton, G. Milgram, and M. E. Meyerson, Eds. New York: The Free Press, 1966.

Schulman, Bruce J. *Lyndon B. Johnson and American Liberalism*. Boston: Bedford Books of St. Martin's Press, 1995.

Schussheim, Morton J. *Housing the Poor: Federal Housing Programs for Low-Income Families, CRS Report for Congress*. Washington, DC: Library of Congress, 1998.

Simon, David, and Edward Burns. *The Corner: A year in the Life of an Inner City Neighborhood*. New York: Broadway Books, 1997.

Skull, Steven A., and M. E. Sharper. *A Kinder, Gentler Racism?: The Reagan-Bush Civil Rights Legacy*. Armonk, New York: M.E. Sharpe, Inc.1993.

Struyk, Raymond, Margery Turner, and Makiko Vino. *Future US Housing Policy: Meeting the Demographic Challenge*. Washington, DC: The Urban Institute, 1988.

Tenement House Department. *First Report of the Tenement House Department of the City of New York, 1902–1903* (Vol. 1). New York: Tenement House Department, 1904.

———. *Second Report of the Tenement House Department of the City of New York, 7/1/03–12/31/05.* New York: Tenement House Department, 1905.

The New York Times, 27 January 1991–5 October 1999.

The Philadelphia Housing Authority. *Building Better Neighborhoods.* Philadelphia, PA: The Philadelphia Housing Authority, 1998.

The Washington City Paper, August 18–24, 2000.

The Washington Post, 29 November 1998–9 November 2000.

University of Pennsylvania, Department of City and Regional Planning. *Rethinking Housing and Community Development Policy.* Philadelphia: University of Pennsylvania, 1977.

US Census Bureau. *Historical Poverty Tables.* Washington, DC: Government Printing Office, 1997.

US Department of Housing and Urban Development. *Programs of HUD.* Washington, DC: Department of Housing and Urban Development, 1967.

US Department of Housing and Urban Development, Office of Policy Development and Research. *A Picture of Subsidized Households, Volume 3, Mid-Atlantic.* Washington, DC: HUD, 1996.

US House Committee on the District of Columbia. *Certain Alleys in the District of Columbia, H.R. 13219,* 63rd Congress, 1914.

US Senate Committee on the District of Columbia. *Discontinuance of Alley Dwellings in the District of Columbia,* 77th Congress, 2nd Session, 1922.

———. *Inhabited Alleys in the District of Columbia and Housing of Unskilled Workingmen.* S. 1624, 2376, 2397, 2580, 4529, 4672, 63rd Congress, 1st Sess., 1913.

Wallace, James E. "The Dilemma of the Disposition of Troubled FHA-Insured Multifamily Rental Property." *Housing Policy Debate,* 5, no. 1 (1994).

Weiner, Jonathan. *The Beak of the Finch: A story of Evolution in our Time.* New York: Alfred A. Knopf, 1994.

White, Graham, and John Maze. *Harold Ickes of the New Deal.* Cambridge, Massachusetts: Harvard University Press, 1985.

William Smith v. Housing Authority of the City of Pittsburgh: Motion for Order allowing the Housing Authority to Proceed with home selection and continue with prioritized transfers. The United States District Court for the Western District of Pennsylvania, 1997.

Willmann, John B. *The Department of Housing and Urban Development.* New York: Frederick A. Praeger, 1967.

Wohl, Anthony S. *The Eternal Slum: Housing and Social Policy in Victorian London.* Montreal: McGill-Queen's University Press, 1977.

Yelling, J. A. *Slums and Slum Clearance in Victorian London.* London; Boston: Allen & Unwin, 1986.

Index

About the Authors

James G. Banks, a native and resident of Washington, DC, served as an official for housing programs at both the local and federal levels for nearly thirty years. He has also been an active community leader, serving on the Boards of Directors of a host of charitable organizations. Since his retirement from federal employment nearly thirty years ago, he has continued his charitable activities and served as a housing consultant. His clients included the Department of Housing and Urban Development and the Federal National Mortgage Association.

Peter S. Banks is a writer living in Washington, DC.